ART CRITICISM

ART CRITICISM

A User's Guide

JOSEPH DARRACOTT

BELLEW PUBLISHING
London

First published in Great Britain in 1991 by
Bellew Publishing Company Ltd
7 Southampton Place
London WC1A 2DR

Joseph Darracott is hereby identified as author
of this work in accordance with section 77
of the Copyright, Designs and Patents Act 1988

ISBN 0 947792 39 2

Designed by John Leath MSTD

Phototypeset by Intype, London

Printed and bound in Great Britain by
Billing & Sons Ltd

for

Ingrid and Jonathan

ACKNOWLEDGEMENTS

My grateful thanks go to Anne Channon, Theo Cowdell, Karin Duckworth, and Gordon Millar for advising on this work while in progress. I should also like to thank my family, colleagues and friends; they will, I am sure, recognise ways in which their influences have improved these pages.

Contents

Illustrations

Illustrations are to be found between pages 60 and 61

Measurements are given in centimetres, height before width

Introduction

This book is about a way of reading art criticism. The method suggested is basically simple. The reader starts by assuming that art criticism is made up of description, interpretation and evaluation. Where these three elements are present, art criticism will be at its most helpful for enhancing the enjoyment or appreciation of art. The reader's method is to discover these various elements in a piece of writing, and then judge their effectiveness.

So, this is not a book for specialists. It is a game anyone can play. Art students and tourists make some appearances in these pages; from this evidence it can be correctly deduced that their needs and wishes have been considered.

As any writer would hope, other possible readers are legion. Long ago there was a fashion for composite photographs, in which the features of several people such as members of a sports team were merged. An amusing example was a book on Gilbert and Sullivan with a portrait which combined the features of the poet and the musician. If a composite portrait of the readers of this book were to exist, it might include a sixth-form student, an undergraduate reading history, literature or perhaps one of the sciences, a graduate taking a new or renewed interest in art, and more than one sort of teacher.

What will these readers find? Besides a method for reading, two key ideas are expressed. First, since writings on art appear in different places, the strengths or limitations of these sites for criticism are outlined. Figs do not grow upon thorns, nor does an evocative description and a detailed interpretation fit into the space available for a newspaper listing. Second, art history may be found within art criticism, and art criticism may be found within art history or various other writings connected with art.

The simplicity of these ideas creates difficulty about using terms, some of which have special meanings in aesthetics, art theory, cultural history or such specialisms as semiotics, to say nothing of art history, which has increasingly drawn on other disciplines for inspiration and new directions. It is worth emphasis that this book is not in competition either with courses in art appreciation or teaching in art history. It is a primer, which supplements such academic study, or which can be read on its own as a means of self-help. The criticism discussed is mainly limited to painting and sculpture, and the book's examples have been chosen to illustrate arguments, not to provide any systematic coverage of artistic periods or styles.

In short, the prospective reader of high theory or historical detail should look elsewhere. This is a book which leans towards helping beginners; it is intended to be useful to any inexpert reader of writing on art.

1

Needles in hay: is it art criticism?

TWO QUESTIONS

What is art? Leo Tolstoy asked the question, and in 1898 his remarkable book with that title gave his reply. He underlined the need for art to communicate what the artist has felt:

> Art is a human activity consisting in this, that one man consciously by means of certain external signs, hands on to others feelings he has lived through, and that others are infected by these feelings and also experience them.
>
> Art is not, as the metaphysicians say, the manifestation of some Idea of beauty or God; it is not, as the aesthetic physiologists say, a game in which man lets off his excess of stored-up energy; it is not the expression of man's emotions by external signs; it is not the production of pleasing objects; and, above all, it is not pleasure but it is a means of union among men joining them together in the same feelings, and indispensable for the life and progress towards well-being of individuals and humanity.[1]

There are many more definitions of art besides Tolstoy's own and those which he denounced. For the purposes of this book, just two assertions will have to content us: first, some works have been intended by their makers to be seen as art; second, there is a consensus today that other works are to be described as art. Since art critics have these working assumptions in mind, and it is with their writing we shall be mainly concerned, we need to proceed without being distracted. We shall not look into the myriad issues springing from problems of definition which are vital for philosophers and aestheticians.

Is it criticism? There is a massive amount of writing about art, only some of which can immediately be identified by a reader as criticism. Writing by the art critic of a newspaper is self-evidently criticism, in parallel with the writing of music and theatre critics; an exhibition can be treated almost in the same way as a performance. Articles in magazines are less certainly described as criticism, for their main topics may be personalities or history, and art may be only a small part of the writers' account. Books and catalogues may contain criticism; but their writers may think of themselves as art historians, philosophers, aestheticians, anthropologists, historians or biographers, and there are many other possibilities; their books may never be identified as art criticism.

As the following chapters will show, the useful and helpful functions of art criticism will receive preference in the choice of what is quoted or discussed. Is the text or part of the text written so that a reader will benefit in a future encounter with a work of art? Some writing which is called art criticism will be helpful, some will not; other writing will also be valuable, although whether it can be described as art criticism may be disputable.

A REVEALING INSTANCE

A famous passage of art criticism can be cited as one example entirely beyond dispute. The author spent much of his life as a bachelor Fellow of Brasenose College Oxford; his cloistered life was devoted to writing, notably on classical antiquity and the Italian Renaissance. Walter Pater was a master of atmosphere; he had been inspired as a young man by Ruskin, and his idealism about art and his fine prose were in turn much admired by a younger generation of aesthetes, among whom Oscar Wilde was a prominent figure. One of Pater's subjects for a perceptive essay was Leonardo da Vinci; it gave special prominence to the painting now generally known as the *Mona Lisa*. The following critical passage comes from this piece, first published in the *Fortnightly Review* in 1869, and then in 1873 in Pater's book, *Studies in the History of the Renaissance*.

> *La Gioconda* is, in the truest sense, Leonardo's masterpiece, the revealing instance of his mode of thought and work. In suggestiveness, only the *Melancholia* of Dürer is comparable to it; and no crude symbolism disturbs the effect of its subdued and graceful mystery. We all know the face and hands of the figure, set in its

> marble chair, in that circle of fantastic rocks, as in some faint light under sea. Perhaps of all ancient pictures time has chilled it least.[2]

Pater's measured prose goes on to connect the picture with drawings by Verrocchio, speculate on the artist and the sitter, and wonder about how long the picture was in progress. Then comes the peroration.

> The presence that rose thus so strangely beside the waters, is expressive of what in the ways of a thousand years men had come to desire. Hers is the head upon which all 'ends of the world are come', and the eyelids are a little weary. It is a beauty wrought out from within upon the flesh, the deposit, little cell by cell, of strange thoughts and fantastic reveries and exquisite passions. Set it for a moment beside one of those white Greek goddesses of beautiful women of antiquity, and how would they be troubled by this beauty, into which the soul with all its maladies has passed! All the thoughts and experience of the world had etched and moulded there, in that which they have of power to refine and make expressive the outward form, the animalism of Greece, the lust of Rome, the mysticism of the Middle Ages with its spiritual ambition and imaginative loves, the return of the Pagan world, the sins of the Borgias. She is older than the rocks among which she sits; like the vampire, she has been dead many times, and learned the secrets of the grave; and has been a diver in deep seas, and keeps their fallen day about her; and trafficked for strange webs with Eastern merchants; and, as Leda, was the mother of Helen of Troy, and, as Saint Anne, the mother of Mary; and all this has been to her but as the sound of lyres and flutes, and lives only in the delicacy with which it has moulded the changing lineaments, and tinged the eyelids and the hands. The fancy of a perpetual life, sweeping together ten thousand experiences, is an old one; and modern philosophy has conceived the idea of humanity as wrought upon by, and summing up in itself, all modes of thought and life. Certainly Lady Lisa might stand as the embodiment of the old fancy, the symbol of the modern idea.

Pater's book is a classic, and easy to find in a library. But if the books are arranged by subject, there is no certainty that *The Renaissance* will be put under 'art criticism'. Several other headings are equally possible, say aesthetics, English literature or Italian history. The library user who looks for books of art criticism is not necessarily going to have an easy task.

Let us picture a girl entering through the impressive doors of the New York Public Library. Her interest has been aroused by some new paintings which she has seen in a SoHo gallery, which a friend has compared unfavourably with the work of Lee Krasner. This comparison has fazed her, as she only knows about Lee Krasner as the widow of Jackson Pollock; so the library visit is intended to check out reproductions of Lee Krasner's work, to see if she has to concede that her friend may be right. The resources available to her are excellent; the library has an extensive stock of books, long runs of periodicals, press cuttings, and up-to-date facilities to find relevant material. Among the sources she will find are critical reviews, articles, catalogues and books about New York painting of the 1940s and 1950s, which will remind her that Pollock died in 1956. There is no shortage of writing about Pollock; like other star artists, he has an embarrassingly large number of apologists, but fortunately there are select bibliographies which can guide her to key publications. There may, however, be questions in her mind about the choices open to her: how will the information in a catalogue differ from what is to be found in a monograph? How much of the books about Pollock will be biography and how much will be about his art? Among the magazine articles, which are most likely to be interesting to her? Will she find good reproductions of Lee Krasner's work?

Our American friend's cousin in London is an art student. Her college library has interesting books, as well as the latest art magazines. Her course teacher has given her a reading list, and the library staff are good at helping students with all sorts of interests. As part of the course, she has to choose a subject of her own about which to write a paper; one of her difficulties is to know how to form her own views, not just copy already received opinions. She is looking for critical views against which to pitch her own; it seems that she may have chosen the wrong sort of topic, since on a holiday in Italy she had been stunned by the newly renovated Michelangelo ceiling in the Sistine Chapel in Rome, and although there were plenty of books about it, many of them went into extravagant detail. Happily her supervisor has guided more than one student through topics about Michelangelo, and has a route map prepared, including introductory and background books, but also passages from longer scholarly works.

If the two girls compare notes one day, the New Yorker will complain about the useless articles she read; the newspaper articles were almost always short, written maybe by hard-pressed critics who were only allowed short articles, further cut down by sub-editors. Still, by reading, and looking at Lee Krasner's pictures in New York galleries, she was able to defend an independent liking for her SoHo artist. In London, it was a rather different story, since the literature available needed discrimination, much of it being historical and iconographic, establishing data of little interest to the art student. To her surprise, there proved to be perceptive judgements about qualities in Michelangelo's work, almost hidden in catalogue entries; more than one art historian, apparently, was not only learned but had an eye.

ART CRITICISM AND ART HISTORY

Do art historians write about the past, while art critics write about the present? Things are not so simple, as some art historians write well about the present, with a generosity of feeling and approach enriching to contemporary culture. They are capable of assessing modern art in its own terms, partly from experience gained through judging work of other periods within quite different terms.

Meyer Schapiro, who had a specialist concern with Romanesque art, was an open-minded historian of this sort. He wrote enthusiastically about the later work of Arshile Gorky: 'Gorky's atmosphere, veiling the hard opaque wall of the canvas, evokes a nocturnal void or the vague, unstable image-space of the day-dreaming mind.' And he remembered the painter:

> I used to meet him most often in the museums and galleries fixed in rapt contemplation of pictures with that grave, searching look which was one of the beauties of his face. As some poets are great readers, Gorky – exceptional among painters – was a fervent scrutinizer of paintings. No interesting touch or invention of form escaped his eye. He was equally at home in the Metropolitan Museum and the Museum of Modern Art, keen in discerning what was good in the arts of many ages and styles.[3]

As for working art critics, their newspapers need reviews of every sort of exhibition, whether modern or historical. Even though critics may not be as learned as their art-historical colleagues, there is no good reason for their practised eyes to cloud over when looking at art of other periods.

Furthermore, artists who are also critics are especially likely to make vivid comments on the methods and techniques of old art. The guards on the frontiers between art history and art criticism shoot neither intruders nor escapers. Indeed, there are some who feel that there should be no border, thinking back nostalgically to days when there was only one domain of art. In some writing today, too, it is possible to find the words critic and historian being used interchangeably. Art is after all the subject of attention for both critic and historian, even though the functions and methods of the two sorts of writer have drawn apart.

Fifty years ago they were in closer touch. It was in 1936 that the first American edition of Lionello Venturi's *History of Art Criticism* was published, containing material which could equally have found a place in a book about art history. Venturi was a university teacher, son of a famous father, Adolpho Venturi, who had made a substantial contribution to the publication of documents of Italian art. Venturi's survey started with classical times, the uncertainties of writing by Xenocrates, lists of lost works such as the treatise by Apelles, and settled down to comment on two fundamental categories of criticism, the lives of artists, and the critic's encounter with the work of art. For the latter he quoted a sentence by Lucian, the second-century Greek rhetorician: 'A work of art requires an intelligent spectator who must go beyond the pleasure of the eyes to express a judgement and to argue the reasons for what he sees.'[4]

For Venturi, an important development in art criticism came in the eighteenth century which saw the foundation of aesthetics and the rise of philosophies for which art was an indispensable ingredient. Writing as he was in the 1930s, he expressed his pleasure at the extensive documentation and reference material available to the student of art, instancing the growth of libraries and art historical teaching. If he were alive today, he would have even more cause for satisfaction.

Some of the main efforts of historians in the first decades of the twentieth century had been directed to putting order into a mass of material, analysing works and documents, and establishing historical data. German art historians had begun much more systematically on this task than others. Several art historians wrote syntheses of art historical information, which became standard works. Histories of art appeared in sequences of volumes by different authors, there were several series of books about artists and on museum collections, besides which the most comprehensive biographical dictionary of artists by Ulrich Thieme and Felix Becker started its long publication process in 1907.

Roger Fry acknowledged German scholarship as a precursor of serious art historical studies in this century. Fry was a connoisseur of Renaissance art, but also he defended Post-Impressionism (a term he invented), was a painter, and published a monograph on Cézanne. In 1933 he wrote as follows in a lecture at Cambridge University:

> An enormous amount of work has been done and perhaps still more remains to be done in arranging works of art in exact sequence of time. It is here that the Germans have done so much pioneer work, and indeed the whole tendency of their art historical studies has been to regard works of art almost entirely from a chronological point of view, as coefficients of a time sequence, without reference to their aesthetic significance.[5]

The title of the lecture in which these words appeared was *Art-history as an Academic Study*, but those were early days for the subject in the British Isles; only in London was there undergraduate teaching, at the Courtauld Institute which opened in 1933. His unusual topic gave Fry trouble with the title of his lecture: 'The mere fact that we have no word to designate that body of studies which the Germans call *Kunstforschung* – a body of studies of which the actual history of Art is only a part – is significant. I am obliged to use the awkward and inadequate word "Art-history" for it.'[6]

Critical appreciation was desired by Fry as a necessary part of a course in art history, and is today naturally included. An English handbook written in 1980 even went so far as to state: 'The enjoyment of looking (what we call the aesthetic experience) is, in fact, the core of the discipline known as Art History.'[7] Later in the 1980s an American handbook took a more comprehensive view:

> The goal of art history is first to place the work of art in history and then assess it in the light of its unique position. Modern art historians strive to analyze, interpret, and evaluate works of art by identifying their materials and techniques, makers, time and place of creation, and meaning or function. They inquire about the who, what, when, where, and why of the art object; often the object itself suggests which of these questions should be pursued. But the function of art history today is not only to make such identifications, but also to relate an individual work humanistically to other works of the same school, period and culture, while remaining sensitive to its salient aesthetic qualities.[8]

According to this American guide, 'Art criticism is a many-leveled activity that comprises the historical, the recreative, and the judicial. In all cases it seeks to pronounce value judgements, an exercise shunned by art history.'

The signs are that the next few years will see some extensive soul-searching about art history; several books have already appeared. From Germany there is *The End of the History of Art*; from Britain a group of essays describe *The New Art History*; from the United States has recently come *Rethinking Art History: meditations on a coy science*; and from Canada there is a forthright title *Art History: its use and abuse*. Art criticism seems more likely to remain in the shadows, out of the spotlight of academic controversy.

WRITINGS ON ART

Apart from art criticism and art history, there exist several other types of writing about art. There is the theory of art, and there is aesthetics; there is writing about artefacts which may or may not be categorised as art, but are in the hands of the archaeologist or the anthropologist; and there is art appreciation. A guide to art reference books published in 1969 had 2,500 entries, some of which referred to series; for example, there was a single entry for the series of monographs on individual artists, called *Klassiker der Kunst*, also published in French as *Classiques d'Art*, in which there are thirty-eight books. This guide was extensively revised over nine years, and was republished in 1980 as a *Guide to the Literature of Art History*, intended for 'persons doing serious research in the field of art history'.

Another sort of writing about art is what artists themselves have written, either about their own work or about other artists. This may be by way of theory, or on more matter-of-fact lines about technique or such questions as composition. Some writing by artists takes the form of instruction; in every period manuals on how to do it, whether drawing, making sculpture or other technical tasks are found, though their incidence is irregular, and such treatises are often the work of minor artists, rather than the great; Leonardo is an exception.

Teachers of art are more likely to write books of instruction, and in their efforts to educate their students may make comments about the traditions they admire and from which they hope their students will learn. One lesson for practical students is to analyse works. A teacher's list for analysing pictures may be something like that of the American educationalist Thomas Munro: first impressions of the picture as a whole, line, light and dark, colour, mass, space, unity of design. Books on art appreciation will also concern themselves with formal questions, as they have done since the beginning of the century. In a book called *How to Appreciate Pictures* by R. C. Witt, written in 1902, the chapter headings are not so different: drawing, colour, light and shade, composition, treatment, methods and materials. A supplementary approach to school art instruction is to draw attention to the types of subject in art, such as portraiture, narrative, landscape. This thematic method is combined in many introductory courses with formal analysis which is closer to the way that many artists describe pictures.

An example of an artist acting directly as a critic is Bridget Riley, who selected a show of pictures from the collection at the National Gallery in London, in a series called 'The Artist's Eye'. Bridget Riley came to prominence as an artist in the 1960s, when her dazzling patterned paintings were a clear success in British Op Art. Her National Gallery choices of pictures were examples of problems posed to artists by colour, and in a video talk she demonstrated how these artistic problems had been solved. Connections with her own practice as a painter were evident, even though her abstract compositions were very different in subject from the works of her chosen artists, who included Veronese and Poussin. Her argument was that the subjects of the old master paintings could be disregarded by a painter who wished to find lessons for the present in the artistic practice of the past. Bridget Riley had no intention of either presenting an account of Poussin's aims and procedures, or of demonstrating Veronese's debts to his predecessors in Venetian art, as a historian would have felt a duty to do.

The artist as critic in this case deliberately avoided the historical context of the pictures she was discussing. Any art critic may take such a position, but a historian almost never. Even if historians are specifically interested in form, it is likely to be the history of forms, or the development of styles which will have attracted their attention. It would be too crude a generalisation, though, to say that critics are concerned with form, while historians are interested in the context of art; both the forms and contexts of art are common ground for the critic and the historian.

The ground has been thoroughly explored over the last 250 years, which is one estimate of the span of art critical and art historical activity. Some authorities might argue for a shorter span, giving Baudelaire a title as father of modern art criticism or Wölflinn the key part in the development of art history. It is in the last hundred years or so that theories have been advanced to justify critical or art historical practice, the creation of such theories being made more urgent in the last fifty years by a struggle to establish and then uphold the status of art history as an academic discipline. The study of Oriental art in the West has fared less well. A firm basis for the study of Oriental art came more slowly, and as we shall see, some of the differences of approach between East and West still require wider recognition. Moreover, other cultures, such as those of Africa, have had to wait until even more recent times for recognition.

It is literature within the last three centuries, then, that provides the main choices for a reader. The advice offered here is that a reader should ignore what category of writing a book or article may come under, since helpful art criticism may be found in all sorts of sources. There is no need to be intimidated by the formality of a staid institution's catalogue, or to neglect popular magazines; as for writing in various academic disciplines, there ought to be no barrier to learning about an interesting topic. The reader's question of a book or an article should be what function the writing is able or unable to perform? Writing of many types may assist a reader who looks forward to an encounter with a work of art.

A RULE OF THUMB

It will by now have become evident that this book takes an unorthodox approach to art criticism. There will be no attempt to define exactly what art criticism is, or to set out a theory of criticism, beyond the suggestions of some differences in writings on art which have already been made. Nor will a history of art criticism be attempted. The stress of the book falls on a viewer's encounter with a work of art, and how a prior reading of a piece of art criticism can improve that encounter. To put the matter in a slightly different way, reading art criticism is a preparation for an aesthetic event. James S. Ackerman, the architectural scholar, makes use of this phrase in writing about art and communication: 'What a work of art communicates can be described only in terms of an interaction between an object and a subject; it communicates nothing at all unless someone is there to look at it. In other words, there are no aesthetic objects, only physical objects, which, when observed, are capable of stimulating an aesthetic event.'[9]

We can return for a moment to talk to the girl who went to Italy, and was overwhelmed by Michelangelo's Sistine Chapel ceiling. Her idea of the value of art criticism was a simple one. In her mind there was a set of events which includes reading about a work of art and looking at it. There was a crucial sequence. Michelangelo painted the ceiling. Critics have visited the chapel and written about it. This writing was discovered by her; she read some material before her visit, which prepared her a little for what she would see. When she came to writing for her college project, she found other material; this will enable her to enjoy the work more fully on a second visit.

In her reading about the Sistine Chapel, we can imagine our friend using a rule of thumb to distinguish what was helpful to her. According to this, art criticism has three indispensable elements. These are description, interpretation, and judgement.

Walter Pater's account of the *Mona Lisa* can be used as an example. The description is rather slender, but Pater was able to assume some existing knowledge on the part of his reader: 'We all know the face and hands of the figure, set in its marble chair, in that circle of fantastic rocks, as in some faint light under sea.' Pater's interpretation is justly celebrated, with its cornucopia of cultural references to Troy, Greece, Rome, the Middle Ages, as well as to Pagan gods and Christianity. It is a memorable evocation, casting a spell over the reader: 'She is older than the rocks among which she sits; like the vampire, she has been dead many times, and learned the secrets of the grave; and has been a diver in deep seas, and keeps their fallen day about her . . .' Pater's judgement is decisive, that this picture is Leonardo's masterpiece.

Art criticism at its most helpful does not stint the reader of any one of these elements. As four chapters will demonstrate, there are different places to find art criticism; a monograph will afford the greatest opportunity for full critical treatment, while a brief newspaper article is most likely to omit one or more of the three helpful elements, perhaps through the writer's assuming prior knowledge on the reader's part. To be aware of the limitations of different forms of publication is an advantage for the reader, who can by this means avoid unnecessary disappointments.

Description, interpretation and judgement are the subjects of separate chapters, where they are considered in more detail. Without anticipating this fuller discussion, it is worth making two or three points immediately. Description is a heading which includes both a description of the work itself and of the critic's response to it. Interpretation is the heading which is the most wide-ranging of the three elements, including questions of form or style, but perhaps additionally considering the work's historical background, and technical, thematic or other questions, including the artist's biography. The evaluation is a summing up which places the work in the experience of the critic, and helps the reader to form a judgement.

The plan of the book, then, is simple. After the first two chapters, it discusses where and how to read art criticism. While this first chapter has outlined what that criticism is, the next gives sketches of half a dozen critical types. So, it is to the critics themselves we turn next.

2

Amusing and poetic: the best criticism

A FATHER OF MODERN CRITICISM

The qualities of a good critic are clear perception, fine sensibility and eloquence. These same qualities are needed by lecturers, so it is no surprise that some excellent critical writings, such as many of John Ruskin's books, were first read out from a lectern. An art critic also needs a gift for persuasion, perhaps rather more than a head for exposition and argument. Evocative description can be an effective weapon in the armoury of a critic, besides which a light touch of wit or some conversational sparkle do no harm.

We can start with Baudelaire, sometimes considered to be a father of modern criticism. He earned this disputable title by his thoughtful approach to critical issues and the undeniable distinction of his critical practice. His writings on art include several reviews of the Paris Salons, which were either published in booklets or in journals such as the *Revue française*. The custom of writing about the Salons was well established, and had inspired brilliant writing by such an important figure in the eighteenth century as Diderot. By the 1850s the tradition had declined, so that Baudelaire was seeking to give new life to a decayed literary genre. He asserted that a modern artist should be in tune with his times, careful to avoid hackneyed subjects.

Typically, a laudatory essay he wrote was called *The Painter of Modern Life* on the subject of the illustrator Constantin Guys; this gifted if minor artist was accurately targeted by Baudelaire as being in the mainstream of contemporary social and political life. Guys' drawings appeared in such papers as the *Illustrated London News*, a very successful venture begun in 1842, the decade which also saw the founding of satirical journals like

Punch or *Kladderadatsch*. The illustrated periodical was a phenomenon of a world which Baudelaire saw as reborn on Guys' paper:

> Natural and more than natural, beautiful and more than beautiful, strange and endowed with an impulsive life like the soul of its creator . . . He is looking for that quality which you must allow me to call 'modernity'; for I know of no better word to express the idea I have in mind. He makes it his business to extract from fashion whatever element it may contain of poetry within history, to distil the eternal from the transitory . . . By 'modernity' I mean the ephemeral, the fugitive, the contingent, the half of art whose other half is the eternal and the immutable.[1]

Modernity also had other manifestations. In his review for the Salon of 1846, Baudelaire wrote: 'To say Romanticism is to say modern art – that is spirituality, colour, aspiration towards the infinite, expressed by every means available to the arts.'[2] The real benefit of reading Baudelaire himself on the art of his contemporaries is the chance of recovering some of the excitement the poet felt. It is an additional pleasure to recognise his prophetic power of divining where the best art was to be found.

Baudelaire argued for modernity, but he also strongly believed that a critic has the right to be partisan. He asserted the plain fact of the existence of differences in taste. In writing about Delacroix, he placed his hero in a pantheon of artists who were acknowledged masters of great decorative painting:

> Which is the greatest of these great men who differ so much from one another? Each must decide as he pleases, according to whether his temperament urges him to prefer the prolific, radiant, almost jovial abundance of Rubens; the mild dignity and eurhythmic order of Raphael; the paradisal – one might almost say the *afternoon* colour of Veronese; the austere and strained severity of David; or the dramatic and almost literary rhetoric of Lebrun.[3]

The critic, too, according to Baudelaire has a right to be independent, and to work without a system 'which is a kind of damnation which forces one to a perpetual recantation'. He wrote:

> The best criticism is that which is both amusing and poetic; not a cold, mathematical criticism which, on the pretext of explaining everything, has neither love nor hate, and voluntarily strips itself of every shred of temperament. But, seeing that a fine picture is nature reflected by an artist, the criticism which I approve will be that picture reflected by an intelligent and sensitive mind. Thus the best

> account of a picture may well be a sonnet or an elegy . . . as for criticism properly so-called . . . To be just, that is to say, to justify its existence, criticism should be partial, passionate and political, that is to say, written from an exclusive point of view that opens up the widest horizons.[4]

THE ADVOCATE

A partial and passionate critic also writing in the middle of the nineteenth century was John Ruskin, as devoted to Turner as Baudelaire was to Delacroix. He may be taken as an example of a first type of critic, the advocate. Ruskin was a deeply observant man, a close student of the natural world, and capable of a profound and subtle interpretation of Turner's art. This is a passage about *The Slave Ship*, painted by the artist in 1840; it comes from *Modern Painters*.

> It is a sunset on the Atlantic, after a prolonged storm; but the storm is partially lulled, and the torn and streaming rain-clouds are moving in scarlet lines to lose themselves in the hollow of the night. The whole surface of the sea included in the picture is divided into two ridges of enormous swell, not high, not local, but a low broad heaving of the whole ocean, like the lifting of its bosom by deep-drawn breath after the torture of the storm. Between these two ridges the fire of the sunset falls along the trough of the sea, dyeing it with an awful but glorious light, the intense and lurid splendour which burns like gold, and bathes like blood. Along this fiery path and valley, the tossing waves by which the swell of the sea is restlessly divided, lift themselves in dark, indefinite, fantastic forms, each casting a faint and ghastly shadow behind it along the illumined foam . . . Purple and blue, the lurid shadows of the hollow breakers are cast upon the mist of night, which gathers cold and low, advancing like the shadow of death upon the guilty ship as it labours amid the lightening of the sea, its thin mast written upon the sky, in lines of blood . . . I believe, if I were reduced to rest Turner's immortality upon any single work, I should choose this. Its daring conception, ideal in the highest sense of the word, is based on the purest truth, and wrought out with the concentrated knowledge of a life, its colour is almost perfect, not one false or morbid hue in any part or line, and so modulated that every square inch of canvas is a perfect composition; its drawing is as accurate as fearless; the ship buoyant, bending, and full of motion; its tones as true as they are wonderful; and the whole picture dedicated to the most sublime of subjects and impressions . . . the power, majesty and deathfulness of the open, deep, illimitable sea.[5]

Ruskin wrote fluently and seriously, often at length. He was a successful lecturer, much in demand, and put lectures together to make up books; certainly a book is the ideal medium for a critic's extended advocacy of an artist. Nowadays appreciations are often condensed, perhaps into a catalogue introduction, or possibly fitted into the preface for a book of illustrations. These sites of criticism are cramping for persuasive advocacy, even if excellent use is sometimes made of them.

The critic as advocate has been fortunate in twentieth-century France, where a climate of culture has brought art and literature together; also art and philosophy, in the case of Jean-Paul Sartre's advocacy of Giacometti, in whose emaciated figure sculptures the philosopher saw a metaphor of human struggle, even, as he wrote in an article in *Les Temps modernes* in 1948, 'the fleshless martyrs of Buchenwald'.[6]

The connections and friendships of Surrealism can also be instanced as opportunities for advocacy. Parisian cultural life between the wars was close-knit; writers and artists gave each other mutual support. At the beginning of Surrealism it was argued that there was no Surrealist painting, but this dogma was soon reversed. Surrealist painting had publicity value, especially when executed by a showman like Salvador Dali, who married the former wife of the poet Paul Éluard. The internal politics of Surrealism were complicated by rivalries and ideological disputes; in the case of André Breton's association with Dali, his earlier support gave way to a denunciation of the artist, who was expelled from the group. Another famous figure, Joan Miró, initially praised by Breton as 'the most Surrealist' painter, later described his Surrealist phase as having lasted only for a matter of months.

A personal friend of an artist may have a real advantage in writing criticism, as he may learn about artistic intentions which are not explained to others. This places a critic in a privileged position, but also with a responsibility to make clear whether views expressed are those of the critic or those of the artist. This distinction can be limpid if the artist is directly interviewed, and the interview is verbatim; but there are problems of evidence with filming and tape recordings, as well as with interviews, since the viewer or reader is unlikely to know how they have been edited.

THE PROGRESSIVE

A second type of critic may be called the progressive. The archetype here is Guillaume Apollinaire, special pleader for modernism before the First World War. Apollinaire has been aptly called a company promoter of the avant-garde, responsible, as it were, for the successful flotations in Paris of Cubism and Futurism. He welcomed the varied responses of artists and writers to modern life, and in his own poetry explored innovations. He believed that Paris was seeing a forward surge in the arts. Writing on painting as early as 1908, before the word Cubism was in general use, he described the plastic virtues as purity, unity and truth, which 'keep nature vanquished'.[7] Apollinaire was not a nature lover, nor did he revere the past: 'One cannot always be carrying one's father's body about. One leaves it to the company of the other dead. One remembers and regrets him, one speaks of him with admiration. And on becoming oneself a father one must not expect one of our children to burden himself perpetually with our corpse.'[8] And in a phrase which is a benchmark for progressive art criticism, 'Truth will always be new'.[9]

Apollinaire's medium for criticism was the article, now for newspapers, now for magazines, one of which, *Les Soirées de Paris*, he edited from 1913. His approach was assertive, and even brought protests from his collaborators. 'The *Soirées* was not created to support the ignorant and pretentious painters with whom you surround yourself only because they flatter you and who, with the exception of four or five, have no talent whatsoever,' wrote René Dupuy.[10] But Apollinaire had taken a path from which he was not diverted. In 1912 he replied to a newspaper feature about Cubism: 'I am happy to repeat, here, what I have never ceased to write; in my opinion, what it has been chosen to call *cubism* is the highest artistic manifestation of our period.'[11]

Apollinaire's book, *Les Peintres cubistes*, gathered together a main body of his critical writing, but his importance was rather more as a participant in Parisian artistic life than as a theorist; his suggestion of four trends in Cubism is not particularly interesting or useful – scientific, physical, and instinctive Cubism are not categories which have survived; meanwhile Orphism has lived on with a different meaning. On the other hand, the critic's lucid evocations of pictures by Picasso or Braque are well worth re-reading. Here is a passage on Picasso:

> The harlequins go in splendid rags while the painting is gathering, warming or whitening its colours to express the strength and duration of the passions, while the lines delimited by the tights are bending, breaking off, darting out. In a square room paternity transfigures the harlequin, whose wife bathes with cold water and admires her figure, as frail and as thin as her husband, the puppet. Charming lilts mingle, and somewhere passing soldiers curse the day.[12]

Against such poetic passages can be put examination marks given out to painters in short reviews: 'Korody: effort well worth attention. Bolz: very interesting effort; Tobeen: fervent attempts towards beauty', phrases which appeared in *Montjoie*, on 18 March 1913.[13]

Between 1905 and 1914 Parisian avant-garde art was not a financial success. It attracted only a few bold collectors such as the American family of Gertrude Stein and her brothers, or wealthy Russian merchants who were unaffected by French bourgeois taste. Like Apollinaire, they saw a rift between the old century and the new. Gertrude Stein later wrote a book on Picasso, in which she put the point like this:

> One must never forget that the reality of the twentieth century is not the reality of the nineteenth century, not at all and Picasso was the only one in painting who felt it, the only one. More and more the struggle to express it intensified. Matisse and all the others saw the twentieth century with their eyes but they saw the reality of the nineteenth century, Picasso was the only one in painting who saw the twentieth century with his eyes and saw its reality and consequently his struggle was terrifying, terrifying for himself and for the others, because he had nothing to help him, the past did not help him, nor the present, he had to do it all alone and, in spite of much strength he is often very weak, he consoled himself and allowed himself to be seduced by other things which led him more or less astray.[14]

In its slightly earlier day, Pointillism had also had a progressive artistic programme. The critical promoter of the work of Seurat and his friends was Félix Fénéon, a subtle stylist who varied his methods according to the work he was describing; he used expository language for Degas, but he dropped logical connection in language, even verbs when discussing Monet's spontaneous art. In arguing for Pointillism, he quoted the scientific treatises consulted by Seurat and even printed mathematical equations.

Fénéon possessed a dry wit, honed to a sharp edge by journalism; he was a specialist in the sort of notes usually titled as 'News in brief', but in France called 'Faits divers' (Sundry facts). He made these three-liners into sardonic comments which undercut the banalities of the newspaper in which they appeared. As a critic, his descriptions of paintings were phrased with exceptional care. For example, this is how he evoked Seurat's scene of the Parisian suburban resort known as *La Grande Jatte*. 'Beneath a sultry sky, at four o'clock, the island, boats slipping past its flank, stirring with a casual Sunday crowd enjoying the fresh air among the trees; and these forty or so figures are endowed with a succinct, hieratic line . . . The atmosphere is transparent and uncommonly vibrant; the surface seems to flicker or glimmer.'[15]

Fénéon, like other excellent critics, was a valued friend of artists, and so he remained all his life even though he gave up writing criticism after a decade of working on the *Revue blanche* from 1893 to 1903. He accepted a position in a dealer's gallery, where Matisse was among the artists who benefited from his judgement. A thumbnail sketch by a friend brings Fénéon to life: 'He did not thrust himself upon you. First of all, he knew how to listen – which is very rare. But at the same time he was both transmitter and receiver, so to speak. He asked questions, and between his questions and the painter's answers, there was a discovery of the painting itself. Even more, there was a sort of mimesis between Fénéon and the artist.'[16]

A friend to artists in England after the war in which Apollinaire had fought was another combatant, the poet and critic Herbert Read. In 1933 Read published an even-handed book called *Art Now*, eclectic in its selection, with discussions of Expressionism, Abstraction and Surrealism. *Art Now* had started life as a lecture series, but Read was a frequent reviewer of exhibitions, and a contributor to the *Listener*, from which some short essays were published under the title *The Meaning of Art*. Read was a progressive without being wholly partisan. He disobeyed Baudelaire's instruction to be partial, or obeyed it only in so far as he took a stand against conservative taste. He did not take sides against Abstraction, even though he was one of the organisers of a Surrealist exhibition in London in 1937. This was difficult to understand for impassioned artists who saw Surrealism and Abstraction as struggling for the soul of modern art.

Read's account of the work of Paul Klee is characteristic. He judged that it would be difficult to persuade readers of the artistry of Klee's art, which appeared similar to children's drawings, so he stressed the work's imaginative content. This passage was written, incidentally, at a time when he was not well informed about Klee's own ideas. It stands as a sympathetic appraisal by a critic who is trusting largely to his own intuitive sense of quality:

> He wants to suggest the exclusive nature of that subliminal world – to dwell there, and to forget the conscious world. He wants to escape to the world of memory-residues, of disconnected images, for that is the world of fantasy, the world of fairy-tales and myths . . . [Klee's art] denies the reality or sufficiency of normal perception . . . The eye of the artist is concentrated on his pencil; the pencil moves and the line dreams.[17]

THE POLITICIAN

A committed critic writes from a social, nationalist or political conviction, which interacts with an aesthetic response to a work of art. The extreme of critical judgement is to destroy the work concerned, as bulldozers destroyed a Russian exhibition of experimental art in 1974; or to forbid an artist to work, as was the practice in National Socialist Germany, where another form of criticism was used in 1937 by making an exhibition of art to be repudiated by its visitors. This exhibition of 'degenerate art' in Munich showed Abstract and Constructivist paintings which were stated to express 'total madness' and the 'height of degeneracy'.

National or political fervour can alternatively be the motor force of remarkable artistic achievements. The murals of Diego Rivera for the Secretariat of Public Education in Mexico City are admitted by the critic Antonio Rodriguez not to be all of an equally high standard, 'but what poet could keep up the same lyrical flow for a thousand verses? Among some of his frescoes there are some which are imprinted on the memory for ever.'[18] In these 239 murals, covering a surface of 1,585 square metres, there are traces of many influences making up a popular and forceful imagery: 'The codices, pre-conquest sculpture, popular art, the study of living people, the colour of nature as well as the paintings of the misnamed Italian Primitives, together with the modern artistic tendencies to which Rivera himself had contributed during his stay in France, all went to form his own peculiar style, which is apparent for the first time in these frescoes.'

This is art, as Lenin wished, for the people. In the USSR itself, art flourished at first in experiments after the 1917 Revolution, but became confined to social utility after 1922. Art was subordinated to a social theory, and the result was 'Socialist Realism', the realistic portrayal of heroic workers and everyday life in a representational style. 'Socialist Realism' has been described by Ernst Fischer as implying 'the artist's or writer's fundamental agreement with the aims of the working class and the emerging socialist world'; in short, this is a stance of political progressivism. Commentary or criticism of such art within the country concerned necessarily takes the same position.

In modern China an attempt has also been made to create a national art, in this instance by partly discrediting tradition. In 1942 Lu Hsun was quoted by Mao Tse-tung as asserting that the aim of a modern Chinese artist should be: 'By selection to accept the historical legacy of Chinese traditional art; to absorb the best style and technique from foreign art; and thus to establish a new national art in accordance with the demands and needs of the masses.'[19] Mao added: 'To study the development of this old culture, to reject its feudal dross and assimilate its democratic essence, is a necessary condition of our new national culture.'[20] The critical distinction between feudal dross and democratic essence subsequently proved difficult to make.

This brief diversion into the cultural and political history of Germany, the USSR and China has been made to emphasise the way that a state may determine artistic production, and thence art criticism. In other political states during the twentieth century, there has been strong support for the view that art should serve a social purpose. This took such forms as the praise of regionalism in the United States in the 1930s, Marxist criticism in London or New York, or Communist positions taken by Italian critics after the Second World War. An English critic who attempted the task of keeping a balance between his political convictions and his aesthetic responses was John Berger, who wrote in the 1950s for the *New Statesman*. He argued against an excessively formalist type of analysis of art, by pointing out how everyday emotions and ideas also affect the viewer of paintings or sculpture. Many of his readers approved his sensitive and appreciative understanding of paintings, though without sharing his political views.

THE COMPILER

A fourth type of critic can be called the compiler, whose criticism is implied in choices for collections or exhibitions. The compiler's main critical medium is the catalogue, and rather less often articles or a book.

Alfred Barr, the first director of the Museum of Modern Art, New York, is exemplary. In 1936, for example, the Museum put on two crucially important exhibitions, on *Cubist and Abstract Art*, and *Fantastic Art, Dada, Surrealism*. For the latter catalogue Barr chose the Surrealist writer Georges Hugnet to write a historical essay, but it was Barr's intelligent advocacy and choice of works that made the show such a significant affair. In place of the aggressive approach of the early years of Surrealism itself, Barr's commentary is in moderated phrases pointing to similarities between Surrealism and works firmly within the tradition of Western art:

> The explanation of the kind of art shown in this exhibition may be sought in the deep-seated and persistent interest which human beings have in the fantastic, the irrational, the spontaneous, the marvelous, the enigmatic, and the dreamlike. These qualities have always been present in the metaphors and similes of poetry but they have been less frequent in painting, which in the past was largely concerned with reproducing external reality, with decoration, or, as in the more advanced movements of recent years, with the composition of color and line into formal design.[21]

On Dada he wrote: 'With robust iconoclastic humor the Dadaists mocked what they considered the sorry shams of European culture. They even attacked art – especially "modern art" – but while they made fun of the pre-War Cubists, Expressionists and Futurists, they borrowed and transformed many of the principles and techniques of these earlier movements.'[22] Barr, in what used to be a general policy for museum curators, was not writing a passionate defence of the work his museum exhibited. Rather, 'the Museum does not intend to sponsor a particular aspect of modern art, but rather to make a report to the public by offering material for study and comparison'.[23]

Barr's European equivalents flourished in the 1950s rather than the

1930s – Jean Cassou at the Musée d'Art Moderne in Paris, Wilhelm Sandberg at the Stedlijk in Amsterdam, Pontus Hulten at the Modern Museum in Stockholm and then at the Pompidou Centre in Paris. These men were taste-makers, whose judgements were important; but the time available to them for writing was limited by the demands of negotiation and administration, so that they tended to write essays more than books, catalogue entries rather than articles.

THE TRADITIONALIST

Some stress has been thrown thus far on modernism and its advocacy, but a traditional critic may write as well or better than a modernist. Our fifth type must therefore be the traditionalist, for whom it is a pleasure to find the past living on in the present. A traditional critic has the advantage of being able to turn to standards and values inherited from the past.

The highest praise can be given to works which match up and accord with these. A traditional critic may be a practising artist; if so, there is an excellent chance that any technical assessment included in a piece of criticism will be thorough. Joshua Reynolds' comparison of Michelangelo with Raphael can serve us as an example:

> Michelangelo's works have a strong, peculiar and marked character: they seem to proceed from his own mind entirely, and that mind so rich and abundant, that he never needed, or seems to disdain, to look abroad for foreign help. Raphael's materials are generally borrowed, though the noble structure is his own. The excellency of this extraordinary man lay in the propriety, beauty, and majesty of his characters, the judicious contrivance of his composition, his correctness of drawing, purity of taste, and skilful accommodation of other men's conceptions to his own purpose. Nobody excelled him in that judgement, with which he united his own observations on nature, the energy of Michelangelo, and beauty and simplicity of the antique. To the question, therefore, which ought to hold the first rank, Raphael or Michelangelo, it must be answered, that if it is to be given to him who possessed a greater combination of the higher qualities of the art than any other man, there is no doubt but Raphael is the first. But if, as Longinus thinks, the sublime, being the highest excellence that human composition can attain to, abundantly compensates the absence of every other beauty, and atones for all other deficiencies, then Michelangelo demands the preference.[24]

Reynolds was here addressing students at the Royal Academy of Arts in London in 1772. It was the fifth of those lectures he gave from 1769 to 1790, known as his fifteen discourses. In them he took 'every opportunity of recommending a rational method of study', and incidentally inculcating his views of sound critical taste; it would have been a brave student who dared to admire Carlo Maratta, after hearing that he had:

> no great vigour of mind or strength of original genius. He rarely seizes the imagination by exhibiting the higher excellencies, nor does he captivate us by that originality which attends the Painter who thinks for himself. He knew and practised all the rules of art, and from a composition of Raphael, Carracci, and Guido, made up a style, of which the only fault was, that it has no manifest defects and no striking beauties; and that the principles of his composition are never blended together, so as to form one uniform body original in its kind, or excellent in any view.[25]

Reynolds was a notable conversationalist, well able to stand up to his friends, who included Samuel Johnson and Edmund Burke. It is in this more informal context that his draft for a sixteenth and ironical discourse should be read. It attacks his constant enemy, the idea of genius:

> Gentlemen: It is with great regret that I see so many students labouring day after day in the Academy, as if they imagined that a liberal art, such as ours, was to be acquired like a mechanical trade, by dint of labour, or I may add the absurdity of supposing that it could be acquired by any means whatever. We know that if you are born with genius, labour is unnecessary; if you have it not, labour is in vain; genius is all in all. It was wittily said by a bright genius, who observed another to labour in the composition of a discourse he was to deliver in public, that such a painstaker was fitter to make a pulpit than to preach in it.
>
> Genius, as it disdains all assistance, so it defies all obstacles. The student here may inform himself whether he has been favoured by heaven with this truly divine gift. If he finds it necessary to copy, to study the work of other painters, or any way to seek for help out of himself, he may be sure that he has received nothing of that inspiration.[26]

Reynolds' weighty irony was wielded with more address than arguments put forward by later traditionalists. But his views were dismaying to one of the readers of his discourses, the poet and artist William Blake. 'Having spent the Vigour of my Youth and Genius under the Oppression of Sir Joshua & his Gang of Cunning Hired Knaves Without Employment & as much as could possibly be Without Bread, the Reader must Expect to Read in all my Remarks on these Books Nothing but Indignation and Resentment.'[27] As to genius, 'Reynolds' opinion was that Genius may be taught & that all Pretense to Inspiration is a Lie & a Deceit, to say the least of it. For if it is a Deceit, the whole Bible is Madness. This Opinion originates with the Greeks' calling the Muses Daughters of Memory.'

THE THEORETICIAN

The last type of critic to be distinguished in the present chapter will be the theoretician. Today, theory is in high fashion at Western universities, and varied in scope. Literary theory, drawing on other disciplines, including semiotics and linguistics, seeks for underlying structures and meanings in literature. The medium of an art critic as theoretician is the magazine or journal article, not necessarily in a publication specialising in art. Theories are interdisciplinary, and the specific quality of a painting or a sculpture may not be spotlighted by the theoretician, whose writing is likely to be long on interpretation but short on description.

A theoretician is well prepared to consider what the most apt questions about works of art may be. There is, after all, a rich plurality of means and intents in a painting. Paul Valéry wrote that a painter:

> has brought together, accumulated and assimilated by means of the physical materials of his art a host of desires, intentions, and conditions coming from all regions of his mind and being. Sometimes he was thinking of his model, sometimes of the mixing of his pigments, his tone, his oils; sometimes of the flesh itself and sometimes of the absorbent canvas. But, though independent, these objects of his attention coalesced, inevitably, in the act of painting when all the discrete, scattered moments, followed up, caught on the wing, suspended or elusive, were in process of becoming the *picture* on the easel.[28]

Even such richness may not be enough for a theoretician. Victor Burgin explained, for example, in *The End of Art Theory* that he was unwilling to be limited to an aesthetic response to 'the *art object*, which in turn is representative of the sensibility of the artist'.[29] He described this aesthetic response as the bed-rock of conservative criticism. For him, critical writing has to take up wider issues than enjoyment of a picture or a sculpture.

A different sort of response to art is to use it as a means of learning more about the society in which it was produced; this may be felt by a theoretician to be more important than to know the artist's intentions, which, it can be argued, are determined by society. Or, the effect of a painting may be compared with those of other means of communication, such as photography, film or television. There is every reason to welcome such studies, though a reader hoping for judgements about quality may be disappointed by a theoretical writer's greater stress on interpretation.

Theorists may also be more difficult to follow in their arguments because of a current of polemic with which a reader may not be familiar. For example, the writing of Rosalind Krauss has mainly been published in two journals, the American *October* and the French *Macuba*, both advancing a special interpretation of twentieth-century art. This stance is partly a reaction against what Krauss saw as a dominant position in American criticism, by which 'the art of the last hundred and thirty years, the art of modernism, is not being well served by writing that promotes the myths through which it can be consistently misread'.[30] Her particular target for attack was the formalist interpretation of abstract art by Clement Greenberg.

Post-modernist interpretations evolved in her articles between 1973 and 1983, and were published in *The Originality of the Avant-Garde and Other Modernist Myths* in 1987. One of the articles is about the abstract artist Sol LeWitt, who was in Krauss's opinion misinterpreted by three critics as serving 'as triumphant illustration of the powers of human reason. And, we might ask, what else could Conceptual Art be?'[31] However, her own reading of this artist's work, and that of his contemporaries such as Donald Judd and Robert Smithson, was that they saw 'a false and pious rationality' as 'the enemy of art'. From her knowledge of the artists' attitudes to their work, she pointed to the part that uncertainties played in the process of making their sculpture.

3

Aerial view: surveys

CHRONOLOGICAL SURVEYS

'The White Rabbit had put on his spectacles, but he did not know where to start. "Begin at the beginning," the King said gravely, "and go on till you come to the end: then stop." '[1] Many art books follow this plan, especially those aiming to take in a national culture or a whole civilisation. Art histories often make an attempt to keep to chronology, although the difficulties include the crucial fact that in art there is no clear sequence of events. Unlike old-fashioned narrative history, art has no decisive battles, no international treaties, and no changes of government. This is perhaps a more useful analogy than might at first sight appear. Newer approaches to history can give accounts which do not have landmark events and which tell us about different aspects of the past, such as social conditions.

Deciding where is the beginning can be a trouble for an art historian. In Europe, classical times are a beginning for historians, but not for archaeologists. For some art historians, the Renaissance is a new beginning, though medievalists can point out convincingly that no one event divides the Middle Ages from the Renaissance. In writings about the Renaissance, its beginning may be seen to waver from the thirteenth to the fifteenth century.

One of the major accounts of the Renaissance in Italy was published in 1860 by a Swiss history professor at Basel University. Jacob Burckhardt sensibly avoids pedantry about a starting date, but stresses the revival of antiquity as a main characteristic of the period. His book entitled *The Civilization of the Renaissance in Italy* avoids a chronological sequence, since his plan of arrangement was to build up a mosaic of characteristic material. As he explained: 'My starting point has to be a vision, otherwise I cannot do anything. Vision I call not only optical, but also spiritual realization; for instance, historical vision issuing from the old sources.'[2]

A more mundane project for a survey writer is to scan Western art, which has often been attempted in series of books, many of them, as Roger Fry's comments implied, by German historians. A few single volumes have had deserved success. One of the best was made out of lectures at the École du Louvre by the French historian Salomon Reinach, first published in English in 1904 (with 600 illustrations). An American work on the same lines was first published in 1926 by Helen Gardner. She called it *Art Through the Ages*. Neither of these works, nor two more which are to be discussed, have attempted to integrate Eastern with Western art.

The limitations of surveys can be demonstrated by two examples of well-respected books. A subtle mind and a firm editorial hand were essential ingredients in the success of *The Story of Art* by E. H. Gombrich, first published in 1950. Gombrich's book is a fine example of a survey, ambitious in scope, clear-sighted in its emphasis on the history of styles, and judicious in appraisals of the work of individual artists. It is relatively brief, as can be seen by comparing it with a more recent competitor for the same market, H. W. Janson's *A History of Art*, which is more than twice the length and has more illustrations (928 in 1962).

Both surveys contain art criticism; Janson uses his advantage of extra space to include more quotations from artists. For example, this is a passage of interpretive description of a Van Gogh self-portrait: '... his emaciated, luminous head with its burning eyes set off against a whirlpool of darkness. "I want to paint men and women with that something of the eternal which the halo used to symbolize," Van Gogh had written, groping to define for his brother the human essence that was his aim in pictures such as this.'[3]

In other passages, the reader may find more difficulty in following Janson's judgement. Here is a passage which shows that a survey can benefit from being used with other books (even though three of the sculptures mentioned are illustrated by Janson).

> Antoine Coysevox, a less self-conscious classicist than Girardon, was another sculptor employed by Lebrun at Versailles. In his large stucco relief in the Salon de Guerre, the victorious Louis XIV retains the pose of Bernini's equestrian statue. Coysevox's bust of Lebrun repeats – again with a certain restraint – the general outlines of Bernini's bust of Louis XIV. The face, however, shows a realism and subtlety of characterization that are Coysevox's own. He is the first of a long line of distinguished French portrait sculptors.[4]

Without comparative material, the reader is in serious difficulty about knowing whether to agree with this three-way discriminative judgement.

Gombrich's scholarly work includes many papers on meaning and interpretation in the visual arts, so that the broad but thin scope of his story of art is instructive; by writing a survey he inevitably limited himself to a narrow range of comment. His book stresses the history of styles, which he describes in sequence, Baroque for example being followed by Rococo, and Neo-classicism. An unwary reader might think that the book is a history of the changes in Western art, whereas it is in fact only a selection of some changes.

The Story of Art highlights change and development, sadly at the expense of art which is less varied, of however high a quality. In other words, stylistic change is at a premium; in Gombrich's book the dramatic innovations of Caravaggio do well, but a distinguished painter, say Bonnard, who is not so bold or challenging an artist was omitted until additions were made to the text in 1971. As for a varied painter, only one work is likely to appear in a survey.

The imperative for a writer of a chronological survey is that a defined period of time is covered; this may be linked with a theme, such as the history of styles in Gombrich's case, but it is unlikely to be linked solely with a spotlight on quality. Excellence is not necessarily a criterion for including a picture or a sculpture in a chronological survey. The author may choose to use a characteristic work, something typical of its time and place. A work of outstanding quality is a pinnacle; it is not typical. There are also technical limitations. A well-known picture book of Italian art alone contains more than 4,000 reproductions, yet histories of art, as we have seen, contain fewer, sometimes much fewer than 1,000 plates. Of the illustrations in any general book relatively few are in colour; a careful author is bound to consider which works suffer least from being reproduced in black and white. Again, the need for the deeply interested reader to supplement a survey with other books becomes evident.

The presenter of a television series has some advantage over a writer, since filming is more flexible than book production. A demonstration of the point is to compare *Civilisation* by Kenneth Clark in its forms as television and book. The television series is a much richer visual experience, and filming has a completely decisive advantage in being able to explore architecture, inside and out. Nevertheless, the limitations of writing a script to accompany images on the screen become clear on the printed page.

The pace of television favours simplifications, generalised statements, witticisms, and short sharp judgements on artists' performances. A presenter, after all, knows that a viewer has the visual evidence to check on what is being said. As for planning, drama is relished in television, no doubt an incentive for Clark to describe the precarious survival of Western civilisation in an episode on the Dark Ages as being saved by 'the skin of our teeth'.

Some commentators have complained that Clark's title, *Civilisation*, was misleading, as only Western arts were treated; but even if Clark had been willing to take on world art, costs would no doubt have prevented such a grandiose project. A single-volume history has recently been courageously and skilfully attempted by Hugh Honour and John Fleming, which inevitably suffers from the problem of compression.

Other civilisations are treated in separate studies. One parallel to the scope of Janson's book on Western art, Sherman Lee's *A History of Far Eastern Art*, was first published in 1964. This contains sixty colour plates and 656 black and white plates. Lee makes firm judgements, as in this comment on a cave painting from the seventh century: 'The most famous figure at Ajanta is in Cave 1 and has been often described as the "Beautiful Bodhisattva". It represents Padmapani holding a blue lotus, and is located at one side of a cell entrance. The figure is much destroyed from the waist down; but the noble torso, and especially the head, express that compassion and humility which is the great achievement of Buddhist art.'[5]

What is true for general histories also applies to surveys of more limited periods. A typical decision for planning a survey is to take a century, or the reign of some sovereign to delimit a period; this is a device with no relationship to the artistic activity of the time. In our rapidly vanishing century, decades are also taken as periods of time to be commemorated. In a dispassionate view, a century seems to have several advantages, as being more than a lifespan and being an evident but arbitrary division. Art is not alone in failing to conform contentedly to such chronological schemes, indeed, some might say that poetry or music are even less amenable.

An alternative to dates is to use a term like Romantic, even if its meaning seems to alter from writer to writer. Who means today what Baudelaire meant? Attempting to capture the spirit of a period is another planning strategy for a survey, though this philosophical notion of a *Zeitgeist* is notoriously elusive. It is perhaps more the stuff of epigrams than analysis. The idea that there is such a thing as the spirit of a time can be awkwardly challenged by asking, 'Whose time?' No prizes can be offered for pointing out that at a given moment there are artists of several generations working and in very different ways.

A further, and rather extreme way of dealing with a chronological survey of art is to eliminate the artists. 'Art history without names' was a phrase used by Heinrich Wölflinn, in his introduction to *The Principles of Art History* first published in 1915. Wölflinn was Burckhardt's successor as professor at Basel, but his later successful career took him to Berlin, Munich and Zürich, a major art historian whose interests were primarily in the Renaissance and the Baroque. Wölflinn was naturally not ignorant of artists, but the famous phrase indicated an interest in the sequence of art seen as forms which develop as if of their own volition. Wölflinn's writings are strong on observation; this can be understood from his choice of terms to describe tendencies in form; linear as against painterly, plane surface as against recessional depth, closed against open form, composite clarity against fused clarity, or absolute clarity against relative clarity. Such polarities were evidently valuable aids to several generations of Wölflinn's pupils who could benefit from his personal teaching as well as the rather more rigid theory in his books.

Wölflinn used such terms to distinguish epochs; they are only partly useful as interpretation, since Wölflinn tended to more interested in art as an independent phenomenon than as having meaning intended by the artist. Wölflinn wrote *Renaissance and Baroque* in 1888, which in the preface he described as follows:

> The subject of this study is the disintegration of the Renaissance. It is intended to be a contribution to the history of style rather than of individual artists. My aim was to investigate the symptoms of decay and perhaps to discover in the 'capriciousness and the return to chaos' a law which would vouchsafe one an insight into the intimate workings of art. This, I confess, is to me the real aim of art history.[6]

In 1964 Peter Murray wrote an introduction to a new edition, in which he made an observation about the passage on Bernini's *St Teresa*, the sculptural group in Rome which is a key work of the Baroque:

> Bernini is evidently attempting to render something quite transcendental and something which had never been attempted by a sculptor before that date. Indeed, it is possible to argue that St Teresa's mystical ecstasies are themselves something entirely new in the spiritual life of Europe . . . Wolflinn himself describes the Bernini statues at some length but at no point does he ever mention the subject . . . Wölflinn was trying to isolate a visual denominator which, he claimed, was common to all works produced at the same time.[7]

The history of forms in art has had some distinguished advocates, some of whom have been concerned with the transformation over time of one form to another; others have been more attracted to problems of values, arguing either that styles in art change and decay, or that in a particular period there is an artistic will to produce work in a style of its own. These are matters which border on philosophy. Eternal values can also be sought in art, as they were by the French art historian Élie Faure, whose open mind accepted disparate arts, a view which he expressed like this: 'It is not paradoxical at all to affirm that an Ivory Coast mask and the ceiling of the Sistine Chapel express the same need to manifest a harmonious rapport which exists between mankind and the universe.'[8]

A reader today can judge the validity of these claims through the means of photography. Extensive records enable us to visit what André Malraux called a *Musée imaginaire*, in which the arts of many cultures and civilisations can be compared. Malraux's books, like thousands of picture books since, emphasise details and similarities across boundaries of time and place. Photographs can reduce the scale of a monument or enlarge a detail for scrutiny. The unfriendly comment of Edgar Wind in *Art and Anarchy* was: 'What has optimistically been called a "museum without walls" is in fact a museum on paper – a paper-world of art in which the epic oratory of Malraux proclaims, with the voice of a crier in the market place, that all art is composed in a single key, that huge monuments and small coins have the same plastic eloquence if transferred to the scale of the printed page, that a *gouache* can equal a fresco.'[9]

GUIDE BOOKS

A tourist may ask many questions about an unfamiliar scene. The answers include history, perhaps technology and sometimes art criticism. There is no shortage of guide books in the modern world, nor of travel books which regale readers with accounts of what travellers have seen. Occasionally a book has almost achieved immortality, like John Ruskin's *Stones of Venice*, but even more modest books can call up the spirit of a place; and a private letter may illuminate both a person and a work of art.

It is easy to sympathise with a traveller who writes: 'I have seen a quantity of things here – churches, palaces, statues, fountains and pictures; and my brain is at the moment like the portfolio of an architect, or a print-shop, or a common-place book.'[10] This is from one of the letters written by Shelley in Italy, which goes on to describe the painting of St Cecilia by Raphael:

> You forget that it is a picture as you look at it . . . There is a unity and perfection in it of an incommunicable kind. The central figure, St Cecilia, seems rapt in such inspiration as produced her image in the painter's mind; her deep, dark, eloquent eyes lifted up; her chestnut hair flung back from her forehead – she holds an organ in her hands – her countenance, as it were, calmed by the depth of its passion and rapture, and penetrated throughout with the warm and radiant light of life.

So vivid a response by a great poet must inspire respect and possibly a curiosity to see if the reader can match the experience.

Guide books customarily take a lesser role, informing the traveller and listing things to see. These functions have been well carried out by Baedeker guides since the foundation of the German firm in the first part of the nineteenth century. Old copies are now collectors' items, with their entertaining instructions and hints. In 1909: 'The unattached cyclist on entering Italy with his wheel must deposit 42 fr. 60c. with the customhouse authorities, which sum is returned to him (though seldom without difficulties) when he quits the country.'[11] Baedeker acquired a reputation for serious standards, and the traveller who missed a double-asterisked attraction had clearly journeyed in vain. Baedeker in 1909, like Reynolds in his fifth discourse, hesitated between two great masters and their works. 'Whether the ceiling of the Sistine Chapel or the Stanze of Raphael should be regarded as the culminating effort of modern art, has long been the subject of controversy';[12] but they both received double asterisks.

A star system in guide books is still common practice today. As art criticism, it has the merit of making a judgement, though description and interpretation may be meagre. Some rankings have more than the approval of the author of a guide, and are attested by other authorities, local or even national. In Czechoslovakia works of importance are graded as national treasures, and while the Japanese have a similar system, they also rank places. For example, the shrine of Miyajima, a temple approached by water through a famous red gateway, ranks number three in Japan.

More informal guidance can be found in books with a personal approach, in which class the *Companion Guide to Rome* by Georgina Masson is exemplary (first published in 1965). There is adequate historical data about the Sistine Chapel, but there is also a personal response:

> More, probably, has been written about this great hall-like chapel than any other building in the world; but in fact no description, picture or photograph conveys the impact which it makes. Perhaps the first, and in the end the most lasting, impression that one carries away, is of the contrast between the golden-cream light and space and the exquisite feeling of harmony engendered by the ceiling as opposed to the deep blue darkness and turmoil of the 'Last Judgment'.[13]

Georgina Masson's special gift was her ability to disentangle and evoke in Rome three different cities, of Classical Antiquity, of the Renaissance, and of the Baroque. Not every city would be suited to this approach, it must be admitted. In Rome a visitor can stand in front of a Baroque church, but a few minutes later, having walked only a short distance, may have plunged back in time to Antiquity. This is not true in Philadelphia, where a new city decisively overwhelms the old. The Liberty Bell and the

Court House are attractions which repay attention, but have far less power of historical recall.

Guide books are arranged to suit the convenience of the traveller, for whom routes round a city or a site are often suggested. In an art museum, the works may be described from room to room, whether in a book or on a sound guide.

A sound guide has an edge over the printed page, since the listener is looking at what is being described, interpreted and judged. However, the limitation of the sound guide is equally evident: only a small number of works can be given such exceptional treatment.

GEOGRAPHICAL SURVEYS

The tourist may find guide books excellent value, but an armchair traveller may be better served in other ways. A favourite choice is a book selected on geographical lines, say on Egypt, Mexico, or China, to mention three civilisations; France, Australia, or Brazil, to take three nations; and Norwich, the Hudson River, or Tuscany to name three areas. Books on any of these topics are likely to have a chronological framework, but the first principle of selection is place. The art discussed may still be *in situ*, or at least in the country of its origin; hence the immense attraction of travel to the sites of great civilisations such as Egypt or Mexico.

Surveys of art on geographical lines are a commonplace of policy for publishers. Among recent successes is the notable Pelican series, whose titles are varied between civilisations (say, Japan), countries (say, France, 1500–1700), and international themes (*Ars Sacra*, about medieval Christendom). The art criticism in such books generally has a slant, questioning whether the country or places have had a determining influence on art. Robert Paine, writing in the Pelican volume on Japan, had an answer:

> There can be no doubt that the climate of Japan imposed on her artists a different attitude towards art problems. The city of Kyoto, the imperial capital, lies surrounded by hills and is frequently bathed in mists. The visibility, lower than that of the drier climate of many parts of China, has caused the artist in Japan to be more concerned with the strength of outline than with the subtleties of depth sought for by his Chinese neighbour. The decorative flatness and the higher colour of Japanese art also follow as products of the same climatic necessity.[14]

Similar passages of critical reflection or speculation can be found in many books. Formal differences in art have been linked to places in varied ways, one of the best-known Renaissance contrasts being the stress on line evident in Florentine art as against the colourist approach of the Venetians, a city on water. Does an English liking for watercolour spring from the country's climate? Does the flat landscape of the Netherlands impose a special sort of vision on Dutch artists?

The reverse of the coin is internationalism, a feature, some might say, of twentieth-century art; not so uncommon either in other periods, where art historians struggle heroically to identify differences between the art of one country and another. Some of these struggles have been inspired by base motives – desires to appropriate art to a national or a political cause. But some such efforts can have sympathy, as in those stirrings of national spirit in central Europe before 1914, when literature, language and music were fuel for Czech, Polish or Hungarian aspirations. Consider Czech art, which might be said to have existed only since the beginning of the Czechoslovak state after the First World War. The beauty and achievements of Bohemian art can perhaps be called Czech only with an effort, but there is no doubt of the attachment of a people to the heritage that they can rightly claim.

Yet Prague was always an international city, whose culture was dependent on native and external traditions alike. Let us walk with a visitor through the city, a veteran of the Second World War who values it as one which was almost unscathed from the bombing which devastated so many European cities. He starts at a medieval Gothic window, a remnant of the first university in central Europe (founded 1348); he pauses at the rebuilt Bethlehem Chapel, the site of where the Mass was first allowed in Czech, and Jan Hus preached before being burnt for heresy in 1413; he pays respects to the relics of the Jewish quarter with its ancient and crowded graveyard; to cross the river he uses the Charles Bridge, lined with Baroque statues (many between 1700 and 1720), and climbs the hill to the Castle where art and architecture of all periods again further embellish the golden city of central Europe. In the evening our friend has supper in the *art nouveau* interior of the Hotel Europe, before going to a performance at the National Theatre, built in the 1880s as a monument to the Czech national spirit, pinioned under the Austro-Hungarian Empire. As he has enjoyed his day, he sleeps soundly without a nightmare about what was specifically Czechoslovak in the sights.

The truth is that nationality in art has limited importance. At no time will this be more true than in the 1990s, when the art critic confronts an increasingly international community of art. Of course, surveys will continue to be written about American painting or German art, British sculpture or Australian print-making; this fact of publication does not mean that these activities have an inner coherence.

Any reader is entitled to ask what purpose such national anthologies serve; their best justification is making art more accessible, enabling those living artists represented to find and hold on to audiences for their work.

The reader can beware of an element of self-interest in such anthologies, whether in the form of books or exhibitions. For one thing, a government agency may have commercial or political aims in commissioning surveys or anthologies. An international cultural agreement is made in parallel with a trading agreement; trade, it is hoped, will follow the art exhibition. Not a new situation, for there are ample historical parallels. For the reader, however, an art defined as national, made as cohesive and marketable as possible, may be less than convincing as an entity; it may be that within a survey or an anthology there are just a limited number of interesting and attractive works.

SURVEYS OF TECHNIQUES

Surveys of technique often include more rewarding art criticism than either chronologically or geographically based books. The writer is able to measure artists not only against each other but also against standards of technical achievement. Here is a passage from a classic work on etching and engraving, about Dürer:

> He was solid, scientific, conscious in all his creating, learning his art from masters who were still in the youth of artistic development, his whole work shows a progress towards an ideal which the trammels of Gothic tradition never left him free to attain without a struggle. By the very energy spent in its realisation, his accomplishment is all the more intense in its expression. He recognised the truest limits of the medium in which he worked, never allowed technical virtuosity to have the better of the central aim of significant composition, and established a balanced style which remains the most perfect model of the line-engraver's art.[15]

The author is the English scholar Arthur Hind. His working life was spent in the British Museum, whose print collection was his special care. He first published a short history at the beginning of the century, but the passage quoted comes from the enlarged edition of 1923. In discussing Dürer, he treated him as the most versatile artist of a triumvirate, whose other members were Marcantonio Raimondi and Lucas van Leyden. Of the latter he wrote, 'Lucas van Leyden is an artist of frailer calibre than Dürer, and prone to lose himself in imitation of stronger men, each of his contemporaries in turn dominating his style.'[16]

Another book about the age of Dürer, but on a different topic, is *The Limewood Sculptors of Renaissance Germany*, by Michael Baxandall, published in 1980. The author started his career in the Victoria and Albert Museum, where there is an important group of this sculpture; his book had a double origin in a museum exhibition and a series of lectures.

Divisions in the book are unusually clear, separate chapters being given to topics such as function, the market, or the historical and political background of the subject. He makes a particular point of technique.

In the chapter on technique the author describes the process of carving a figure from a wood with particular properties. First the hard heartwood was removed, making the intended figure hollow at the back; the sculptor avoided solid masses, unstable in wood (though preferred by sculptors in a material like sandstone); finally in the carving, forms were decided partly to avoid the hazards of the sapwood shrinking and splitting. Limewood is contrasted with oak, and the chapter finishes:

> The properties of the material made limewood sculpture a special medium. It was a medium of the grand form and of the surface, whether polychrome or monochrome; it was not a positive medium of the middle forms, like oak, or even usually of the asssertive instrument, as bronze can be. The grand form offered a scale of more or less assimilation to the form hidden in the wood, the surface a scale of textures, on both of which the sculptors played, and they are a source of specific qualities of the genre.[17]

A final chapter is devoted to four case studies: Michael Erhart of Ulm, Tilmann Riemenschneider of Wurzburg, Veit Stoss of Nuremberg, and Hans Leinberger of Landshut. These short studies are in part historical, but partly art criticism; the study of Leinberger is particularly relevant, as it comments both on an encounter with a sculpture and the problems of reading about it.

> The best preliminary plan may be for the reader to open the book upright at [the illustration] and then go to the other side of the room, to be imposed on from a distance: it is the nearest the book can offer to the proper first encounter with the figure. There is no one way of looking at a sculpture by Leinberger and similarly there is no one angle or distance from which we see it anything like whole, but there is something like a normal sequence of approach. This begins with the figure impinging powerfully from a distance, in this case as one walks into St Martin's at Landshut, more powerfully than other things in the field of view. What carries most punch here is, of course, the gilt y-shaped motif of the folds offered by the Virgin's mantle . . . to stretch a phrase, a Leinberger sculpture is a permanent possibility of cumulative sensation. For, once we have made the first approach to the Landshut Virgin and acquired a first set of impressions, the changeableness of the figure begins to work on us further, now less in the dimension of greater or lesser distance and more in the angle of view.[18]

In comparison, 'One's relation to Riemenschneider's Altar of the Holy Blood is a little passive: one waits and the shift of light will change its mood and meaning.'

This extended critical evaluation is a rarity in a survey, but very welcome in the way it spells out a connoisseur's response in formal terms to a work of art. It has the added value of being firmly rooted in a thorough understanding of technique. Surveys of painting, it has to be admitted, are more fallible in this respect, partly because of the relative simplicity of the means used. Differences exist between the media of tempera and oil, or oil and acrylic, but they do not have the importance of contrasts in other material processes. Nevertheless, there is one group of surveys of painting which have a special interest: those which form part of handbooks or, more grandly, treatises on how to paint. A practitioner's assessment of other artists' work, often in the light of making similar attempts, can make intriguing reading.

Drawings are quite often given survey treatment. The specialist field of old master drawings has received extremely detailed study; the drawings are interesting both in their own right and as a means of knowing more about artists' practices. The connoisseur also hopes to have in a drawing an authentic work by an artist's own hand, which in the case of an oil painting may not be so assured. European studio practice from the Renaissance to the nineteenth century included the master's employment of assistants, and the use of specialists for parts of pictures, such as drapery or landscape.

Watercolours are also treated in surveys. Here the writer is likely to be a practitioner, and the approach may defer to the popular. of the medium as a pastime for amateurs. Print-making has had the advantage of some careful scholars, but an excellent book is by a practitioner, Stanley Hayter. It is modestly titled *About Prints*. In it this English master print-maker wrote lucidly and well about the range of possibilities in his profession. His memories of his Paris studio add spice to his account, for the facilities there were used not only by his students but in addition by such major artists as Miró and Picasso.

The technical survey is above all a category of book in which the writer will have closely observed the material discussed. This observation has direct bearing on questions of authenticity, since a detail may be the way that the true can be separated from the false. William J. Ivins was curator of prints at the Metropolitan Museum from 1916 to 1946. In *How Prints Look*, first published in 1943, he wrote 'an elementary introduction to the appearances (the outward and visible signs) of prints', and cautioned that: 'Most of the time spent over it should be given to looking at its pictures.'[19] The caption material under two images reads as follows: 'In the middle nineteenth century, before photography was in general use, Pilinski of Paris was famous (and notorious) for the deceptiveness of his copies of old woodcuts. This is an enlargement from an original fifteenth-century woodcut. On the opposite page is Pilinski's wood-engraved copy.' 'Pilinski had to redraw his copy of the old and valuable original because he could not paste the original on his block and engrave through it. Every line is different – every line is stupid – and the whole character has changed. In a number of places Pilinski completely misunderstood the "indications" of the original.'[20]

THE SURVEY WITH A THEME

Themes in art have a fascination, since they add a subject interest to a viewer's enjoyment of artistic qualities. The portrait is an endlessly interesting example, a theme redolent with social connotations and artistic references. In Dostoievsky's opinion, 'The portrait painter seeks the moment when the model looks most like himself; in the capacity to find and hold this moment lies also the talent of the portraitist.' The novelist in search of character thus finds a fellow-worker in the painter.

This hope for a natural quality in portraits, however, is frequently disappointed, since many sitters are eager to be flattered. A powerful sitter may also impose a requirement that the portrait looks impressive, so that an amused spectator can look for traces of the consequent power struggle in a picture; Queen Elizabeth I of England was as firm as the Emperor Augustus about the principle that a ruler's actual appearance matters less than the imprint of authority.

The artist's self-portrait is a special case in portraiture and deservedly part of the collecting policy of art museums including the Uffizi, Florence. A successful description of a self-portrait may not be difficult, but an illuminating interpretation may call on many references, especially other artists' pictures of themselves. What can be deduced from a self-portrait is often controversial; a critic is especially likely to read into a self-portrait some opinion held about the artist. When, as in the cases of Rembrandt and Van Gogh, there is a whole series of pictures to choose from, books can be written on the self-images of one artist alone. This theme is a useful one for assessing the quality of a critic's writing, since it tempts the rash into speculation, while an impoverished eye will miss relevant and useful comparisons.

A theme where personal psychology is necessarily absent is the Christian subject of the Madonna and Child. Again, much interest attaches to interpretation, as an impassive hierarchical image of the Madonna is softened through the centuries into a more human and tender figure. The multitude of Madonnas for Italian worship in the Renaissance made this a fruitful theme for connoisseurship which has taken on the task of distinguishing authentic works from those by followers or copyists.

An art critic may have difficulty in deciding how far the picture needs to be considered as devotional imagery, and how far discussion can be limited to artistic merits. An extremist view expressed by a twentieth-century artist is what Matisse had to say about his responses to murals by Giotto. 'When I see the Giotto frescoes at Padua I do not trouble to recognise which scene in the life of Christ I have before me, but I perceive instantly the sentiment which radiates from it and which is instinct in the composition in every line and color. The title will only serve to confirm my impression.'[21]

In a different context, but also on the issue of religion, an American book on the Aztecs by the archaeologist Vaillant commented tartly:

> The Aztecs did not have a term for 'fine arts', nor did they speculate about aesthetics, nor make objects to be contemplated for their beauty alone. They had none of the socially sterile attitude towards art which we adopt in our own culture. Instead, they recognised the value of superior workmanship and used its products to honour the gods who were intermediaries between man and the infinite power of the universe.[22]

The list of themes and their varied fortunes is a long one. For example, landscape painting had only a gradual success as a theme in European painting. Kenneth Clark demonstrated this development of an evolving sensibility to nature in his lectures, *Landscape into Art*, published in 1949. His introduction remarks, incidentally, that:

> anyone who expects this book to be a treatise on the history of landscape painting will be disappointed . . . in spite of copious rewriting, lectures these pages remain. One may remove the words 'next slide please' from the text, but not from the sequences of thought. The publication of lectures is a well-known form of literary suicide. I indulge in it now because the audiences who heard them endured, with much patience, extremes of heat and cold. I am grateful, and can only show my gratitude by giving them the text to criticise under more agreeable conditions. [23]

A characteristic two pages of the text are given to Corot's landscapes, five pictures being cited, though the reader is less fortunate than the lecture audience, as only two are illustrated. Here is Clark's description of Corot's late style:

> From all his great range of delicate visual experiences Corot came to be satisfied with one – shimmery light reflected from water, and passing through the delicate leaves of birches and willows. He concentrated on it because he loved it, and he thereby proved once

> more his extreme simplicity of character. For he had revealed one of the eternally popular effects of nature, one which is still quoted by simple people as a standard of visual beauty.[24]

Animals make up a category of painting with an uneven reputation, though the theme is one of obvious importance and interest in sculpture. *Animal Painting in Britain* was the title of a book by Basil Taylor, where he explained in his first chapter that the topic had been neglected since it was either assumed to be about sporting pictures, or about pictures of horses by such specialists as Sartorius. He quoted the dismissive comment of the writer of the volume on *British Painting 1530–1790* in the Pelican *History of Art*: 'To discuss the Sartorius tribe and such painters is no business of the historian of art, no matter how bitter the accusations of neglect are wont to be from those specialist writers who sometimes confuse the history of art with praising famous horses.'[25] Such a frank exclusion from the domain of art is not a solitary instance.

Exclusion, though, is rather less general a problem than a low status for some categories of painting. Academies of art, whether in the West or in the Orient, have had lists of priorities in themes of art, in which there are many similarities. For example, in twelfth-century China, a catalogue of the Imperial collection had ten headings: Taoist and Buddhist subjects, human affairs, palaces and other buildings, foreign tribes, dragons and fishes, landscapes, animals, flowers and birds, ink bamboos, and finally vegetables and fruit. This sort of listing is worth knowing by a reader, who may occasionally notice that it underlies the degree of attention being paid to a theme by a critic.

THE SURVEY WITH A THEORY

The last type of survey to be considered has a basis in theory. If a critic has a very decided political or religious point of view, this can override other considerations in judgements about art; the viewpoint may also give a bias to the description or interpretation made. A remarkable Marxist interpretation, for example, was made of Florentine painting from Giotto's time to the fifteenth century, by Frederick Antal in the 1940s. Later writers, even those sympathetic to Antal's thesis, have admitted that the argument about class conflict in the period was exaggerated, but this does not exclude the possibility that an equally unexpected approach may not throw light on some apparently exhausted topic.

Of course, a theorist may damage an argument through bias, perhaps excluding relevant evidence inconvenient to the case being made; but this is not a danger exclusive to theorists. Omissions are most patent perhaps in surveys made with a political bias. We have already mentioned in passing the state policies regarding the arts in Germany, the USSR and

China; there have been writers who followed the party lines by giving attention to those artists favoured by patronage, while neglecting others.

A recent survey with a viewpoint is by the American art historian, Whitney Chadwick. *Women, Art and Society* is a synthesis of work that has been progressing for twenty years about women and the visual arts. Some women have acquired status as heroines; Rosalba Carriera, Angelica Kauffmann, Rosa Bonheur, Berthe Morisot, Paula Modersohn-Becker and Käthe Kollwitz have found places in a pantheon of major talent from which there ought never to have been any question of their exclusion. But Chadwick makes some sensible points about the questions raised by her account which challenge common assumptions about art and society. Some are connected with writings about literature, philosophy and politics which are called post-modern or post-structural.

> Post-structuralist texts expose the role of language in deferring meaning and in constructing a subjectivity which is not fixed but is constantly negotiated through a whole range of forces – economic, social and political. They have undermined long-cherished views of the writer or artist as a unique individual creating in the image of divine creation (in an unbroken chain that links father and son as in Michelangelo's God reaching towards Adam in the Sistine Chapel frescoes), and the work of art as reducible to a single 'true meaning' . . . Now artistic intention can be seen more clearly as just one of many often overlapping strands – ideological, economic, social, political – that make up the work of art, whether literary text, painting, or sculpture.[26]

The most difficult theoretical surveys are those which seem to promise to answer difficult questions about art in general, perhaps especially in the modern world. As in books on the philosophy of art, or aesthetics, many do not in fact contain any art criticism, in the sense of description, interpretation and judgement of individual works. Their strengths are rather in clearing the ground of preconceived ideas about the arts, and putting new points of view. When works of art are described only those aspects of an image important to the argument are included. It is in this arena that some of the fiercest intellectual fighting about art is taking place, though the contests range wider than the visual arts to politics and economics. For example, Chadwick states: 'There can be no simple category defined as "feminist art history" ', since the effect of new ideas is that 'much recent scholarly writing has shifted attention from the categories "art" and "artist" to broader issues concerning ideologies of gender, sexuality, and power'.[27]

In short, from some books the reader may gain moral or political enlightenment, but will be disappointed of developing a personal taste. David Talbot Rice describes such development of taste as follows:

> It is far better to like and admire something that is wrong, or to like and admire for the wrong reason, provided we do so sincerely, than to follow slavishly the dictates or ideas of some other person. If our admiration be true, genuine, and progressive we will in the end come to admire the good and cease to admire the bad. We will learn by our own experience what is best, and not by following the dogmatism of another. But a subtle critic may well save us a great deal of time, pain and trouble in the learning, for he can set us aright at the outset, and by his example rather than by his assertions show us how to avoid admiring that which is unworthy.[28]

4

Zooming in: the monographs

MONOGRAPHS ON PAINTERS

Dictionaries describe a monograph as an account of a single subject; by this definition monographs make up one of the most common categories of art publishing. A book on a single painter, for example, is a monograph. There is some doubt in a grey area of differences between monographs on the one hand, and catalogues or biographies on the other. For convenience, biographies will be included in the present chapter, while catalogues will be treated in the next.

There is a boom in publishing books about individual artists, especially those who are already well known. The potential reader of a monograph on a minor artist may not find a book easily, but there are plenty of publications on Leonardo, Rembrandt or Picasso. It might be thought that this was a natural consequence of the popularity of great artists, but in fact the economics of publishing result in some bizarre decisions about art books. The reader with a love of art is not always at the front of a publisher's attention.

Art books are expensive to produce, especially if they contain colour illustrations. One way for a publisher to finance the publication of an art book is to act with other publishers who will share costs; an alternative is to find a subsidy. Both these strategies affect choices of subjects for art books. Other publishing houses in other countries will naturally prefer artists who are already internationally well known. Subsidies are available from a limited number of sources, such as government agencies, charitable foundations, and, today very rarely, private individuals; there is a factor of prestige to be counted in this sponsorship, mediated by the decisions of committees.

This aside, when the reader has found a monograph, what will it contain? An older book, that is one published before around 1900, will only have black and white plates, which are unlikely to be photographs. This applies, for example, to the book on Delacroix published in 1885, selected by A. Robaut and with an essay by Ernest Chesnau. By the 1920s a characteristic book, as for example *Cézanne: a study of his development* by Roger Fry, published in 1927, had black and white photographic illustrations only. In either case, the absence of colour gave an incentive to the authors to provide evocative descriptions. These descriptions were vital to writing about these two artists in whose work colour plays so important a part.

At the end of the twentieth century, at least some colour illustrations are likely to find places in a monograph. They may, however, not be exactly what the author would have preferred, as a colour plate which is readily available (perhaps having been used in another publication) is much cheaper to use than a new plate which has to be commissioned. The reader can thus be aware that a writer may have written round what happens to have been offered. This may be important in assessing how well a writer illustrates an argument.

The standards which can be obtained in colour reproductions today are high, but not always attained. Comparison of illustrations of the same picture in several publications will demonstrate this truism, while the best test of looking at a reproduction in front of the picture itself can be a disheartening experience. A lecture audience looking at a slide projection, incidentally, may also suffer from seeing distorted colours, though art museums take some care to sell transparencies of a satisfactory quality.

Considerations of illustrations aside, the reader will be hoping for enlightenment from the text. It is probable that this will have much to offer. Monographs are a main source of considered art critical writing. The author has had time to consider and reflect, so that descriptions, interpretations and evaluations will have been carefully formulated. There are many choices of arrangement and treatment available to a monographer. An art historian may choose to elucidate the social context of the art, or trace its sources in the work of other artists; these choices will be reflected in the illustrations as well as the text, while sketches, other versions of pictures and related material will be available for the reader to make comparisons.

Roger Fry, in writing about Cézanne, took a different route. A painter himself, he was attracted to the problems he believed that Cézanne had faced and solved in composition and technique. Fry's opening words are: 'Those artists among us whose formation took place before the war recognise Cézanne as their tribal deity, and their totem.'[1] Fry thought that in Cézanne's mature work:

> The ultimate synthesis of a design was never revealed in a flash; rather he approached it with infinite precautions, stalking it, as it were, now from one point of view, now from another, and always in fear lest a premature definition might deprive it of something of its total complexity. For him the synthesis was asymptote towards which he was for ever approaching without ever quite reaching it; it was a reality, incapable of complete realization.[2]

An example of Fry's description of Cézanne's development dealt with colour:

> When Cézanne uses colour we note that at each nodal point of the interplay of planes, Cézanne marks this sequence by a series of small washes of various colours, modulating generally from violet to greenish, or bluish grey. His aim in this was as far as possible to translate changes of tones into changes of colour, feeling that only by this method could the full saturation and pressure of colour be realized.
>
> I cannot doubt that this peculiar method which gave such valuable results in water-colour, influenced Cézanne to apply it at least to the early stages of his oil paintings, and that gradually it grew to be his habitual practice in the succeeding period.
>
> In proportion, then, as we advance in the chronological sequence of his works, we find his material become less and less pastose, his touches more and more liquid and transparent, more like water-colour. The change is gradual. Nor is it so regular that we can trust to it altogether to fix the exact date of any given work. There are returns to the impasto, but thin painting certainly predominates towards the end of the century.[3]

From description to formal interpretation, we can cite part of an analysis of a portrait, *Monsieur Geoffroy*:

> Its success must be partly due to the extraordinary number of sittings to which his admiring and clear-sighted sitter submitted. The construction here is more erudite than in the *Madame Cézanne*. It is less removed from the ordinary conception of a portrait arrangement. The movements here are more complex, there is a less complete frontality of presentment and symmetry of design. The equilibrium so consummately achieved results from the counterpoise of a great number of directions. One has only to imagine what would happen if the books on the shelf behind the sitter's head were upright, like the others, to realize on what delicate adjustments the solidity of this amazing structure depends . . . He it was who first,

> among moderns at all events, conceived this method of organizing the infinite complexity of appearance by referring it to a geometrical scaffolding. Though it must be remembered that this is no *a priori* scheme imposed upon the appearances, but rather an interpretation gradually distilled from them by prolonged contemplation.[4]

Whether Fry was justified in his interpretations of Cézanne is not our present question. What is valuable is to see that here is a critic writing at the top of his bent. And Fry was straightforward about his own perceptions. 'The critic, I hold, should be loyal enough to his own impressions to confess to what is probably due to his own defects. I must admit therefore that there is one passage in this otherwise consummate design [*A Fruit Dish*] of which the meaning escapes me. I cannot see the necessity of the shadow cast by a half-opened drawer in the kitchen table.' It is encouraging to find Fry underlining a point about critical writing – that with a description of a work of art it can be useful to be given an explicit account of how the critic responds. Another point is also made explicitly: his difficulty is assessing Cézanne's work at the end of the century. 'It is more difficult to be precise about this than about the earlier phases, partly because the pictures are rarer and less accessible, and have not been adequately photographed, partly because it includes considerable variations.'[5]

Fry's book contains rather little biographical information, the focus being firmly on Cézanne's work. There is almost nothing about the artist's contemporaries. This not an invariable pattern for monographs, but readers can usually expect that the central figure of a book will receive prominence at the expense of any other artists. If comparisons are included they may be with an artist whose work is considered by the author to be inferior to the subject of the monograph.

Biographical information is another issue. A biography is not a monograph, and, indeed, there are biographies of painters which do little justice to art. In such books the artists' incidental activities receive undue emphasis. The question of what balance can be attained in a book is a familiar problem to literary critics, who are divided in their views into at least two camps, one favouring attention being paid mostly to the text itself, while the other prefers to take other questions into account, including the effect the writer's life may have on the text.

Some see the conflict as having been crystallised by Proust, who wrote an attack on the critic Sainte-Beuve in 1908 (though it was not published until 1954). Sainte-Beuve, as one of the most widely-read critics of the late nineteenth century, had perfected a conversational essay in which personal anecdotes, quotation, literary judgements and reflections were intermingled. Proust took the view that writers should be judged by their works alone, rather than be interpreted through biography. Ironists reflect with pleasure that nevertheless one of the great literary biographies of the century has subsequently been written about Proust.

How valuable biographical information is to literary or art criticism is a question that will never receive a decisive answer; but a commonplace observation can be made, that circumstances alter cases. Some artists separate their art from their lives, some are articulate about their aims, others are gruffly evasive. Cézanne was not forthcoming in his letters or his conversation. His dealer Ambroise Vollard wrote a book of reminiscences about the painter, including a famous passage about his portrait. 'After a hundred and fifteen sittings, Cézanne abandoned my portrait to return to Aix. "The front of the shirt is not bad" – such were his last words on parting.'[6]

The personal characters of artists cannot be infallibly deduced from their work. 'Art is a rum business', thought Turner, and the attentive reader of a book about artists called *Born under Saturn* cannot avoid thinking that artists are unpredictable while reading through its sections on misers, criminals, celibates, debauchees, suicides, melancholics and eccentrics. The authors are Rudolph and Margot Wittkower, and their theme is that while some artists succeed in financial and social circumstances without strain, other artists tend to Saturnine temperaments. 'Saturn is the planet of melancholics, and Renaissance philosophers discovered that the emancipated artists of their time should have the characteristics of the Saturnine temperament; they were contemplative, meditating, brooding, solitary, creative.'[7]

Comparable ideas about artists can be discovered in other cultures, but also very different views. Even in Europe, Saturn is not the only planet under whose influence it is possible to be born. 'Mercury is the patron of cheerful, lively men of action. According to ancient tradition, craftsmen, among others, are born under his sign.' Beyond which, a disbeliever in astrology can find quite other ways of categorising artists.

A final caution about using monographs about painters is that they can seldom be read alone. Historical background is only compressed in a monograph; biographical material may be more extensive in other sources; the painter's contemporaries will not receive much attention, and may be slighted. Even illustrations may not be adequate, details of pictures often being poorly represented, leaving an artist's techniques, materials and handling to be discovered from more specialist studies. The reader can hope, all the same, that the writer will give an account of the special merits of key pictures, and it is these art critical passages which can be of most help in enjoying or appreciating the chosen artist's achievement.

BIOGRAPHIES

A biography of an artist is a tricky proposition for a writer, since the artist may prefer to be judged through art, not life; the incidentals of an everyday activity, not altogether under the artist's control, are rather unimportant compared to the artist's concentrated effort to create paintings or sculpture. The biographer may come up against problems of concealment, both written records and works having been destroyed. Early work is often missing from an artist's oeuvre, while student work or juvenilia may be saved only by chance or possibly by a devoted family.

Lionello Venturi considered lives of artists made up a basic category of art criticism, buttressing his opinion with accounts of writings by Vasari and others. However, if biographies of artists are carefully examined, it will be found that they do not necessarily contain much art criticism at all; a biographer may prefer not to express personal views about the artist's work; a book's main thrust may be to describe the artist's own aims and ideas. This will result in the book evading the task of art criticism altogether, though the critical views of the artist may be recorded. A deferential biographer is especially likely to take this line.

An exception may be illustrated by a passage from a classic biography, that of John Constable by Charles Leslie. Leslie was himself a painter, and thus comments in his own right on his friend's art, as here on a painting of Hampstead Heath:

> I have before noticed that what are commonly called warm colours are not necessary to produce the impression of warmth in landscape; and this picture affords, to me, the strongest possible proof of the truth of this. The sky is of the blue of an English summer day, with large, but not threatening, clouds of a silvery whiteness. The distance is of a deep blue, and the near trees and grass of the freshest green; for Constable could never consent to parch up the verdure of nature to obtain warmth. These tints are balanced by a very little warm colour on a road and gravel pit in the foreground, a single house in the middle distance, and the scarlet jacket of a labourer. Yet I know of no picture in which the mid-day heat of Midsummer is so admirably expressed; and were not the eye refreshed by the shade thrown over a great part of the foreground by some young trees, that border the road, and the cool blue of water near it, one would wish, in looking at it, for a parasol, as Fuseli wished for an umbrella when standing before one of Constable's showers.[8]

Such a passage is exceptional in Leslie's book, which, in the Victorian manner, was a memoir with extensive quotations from Constable's letters. Constable's own personality and opinions are thus the main gain of a reader from Leslie's book. To borrow a phrase from a biography of Van Gogh, the writer had had the advantage of having the artist as a co-author.

This phrase comes from Carl Nordenfalk's book, *The Life and Work of Van Gogh*, first published in 1943 (in English in 1953). Nordenfalk starts his preface as follows:

> Van Gogh's life has so often been made the subject of literary treatment that the art historian is strongly inclined to leave the biographical matter severely alone and concentrate exclusively on the artistic aspect. But he is soon forced to the conclusion that in this case it is impossible to keep the aesthetic side entirely apart from the biographical. The reason is that with Van Gogh art and life are not merely conditioned by each other to a greater degree than with any other artist, but actually merge with each other. In a sense, Van Gogh's life is itself an artistic creation.[9]

Van Gogh as the subject for a biographer is thus a test case. Nordenfalk's book includes the scrupulous examination of visual evidence always welcome and often found in writing by a museum curator. Here he describes the impact of Impressionism on Van Gogh's work in the spring of 1887:

> He had resolutely abandoned his old palette and the method of mixing complementary colours to dirty intermediate tones of grey. Instead, he put a rich range of clear rainbow colours on his palette, replacing the dirty ochre colours with light and more luminous chromium colours, with the addition of Veronese green, ultramarine and lacquer colours, and following the Impressionist recipe in not mixing these colours with anything except white or closely allied colours.[10]

Interpretation of the artist's work, however, depends on the artist's own account, since Nordenfalk had 'the deliberate intention of presenting Van Gogh the writer and thinker'.

The sober intentions of his book were very different from the novels, plays and films which have created a mythical figure in modern culture of the artist as isolated and neglected, recognised only after his death, and whom the phrase 'genius and madness are near aligned' seems to fit. The novel *Lust for Life* by Irving Stone, published in 1934, is the most famous of these productions, popularising a vein of interpretation established early in the century by some of Van Gogh's first advocates, such as the taste-maker Julius Meier-Graefe, who defended Van Gogh in 1906, and went on to write a book in his praise in 1921 called *Vincent*. But this was a drama, the story of the circumstances of Van Gogh's life; 'No attempt has been made,' wrote Meier-Graefe, 'to make a critical analysis of the pictures, which enter upon the scene only in so far as they concern the drama directly or indirectly.'[11]

ARTISTS' OWN WRITING

Van Gogh is famous not only for his art, but for his writing. He did not write an autobiography, but his letters have been a source of fascination to a wide audience, especially artists. Luckily, he had a correspondent in his brother Theo in whom he could confide and with whom he could explore ideas about art; the letters are thus an invaluable source of interpretation. From the distance of a century, some of Van Gogh's enthusiastic appraisals of the art of his time look curious; but then, this artist acting as a critic was especially vulnerable to admiring art with a moral purpose, or work from which he was able to draw inspiration.

Private letters are like a conversation overheard, often more revealing than an autobiography, or than a diary which may have been written with more than half an intention of allowing it to be published. What private letters from an artist can do best is to elucidate what was uppermost in an artist's mind at the time, often artistic aims which would be difficult to discover otherwise. Besides which, there are some artists whom it is a pleasure to know even a little better from their letters.

Many readers must have sighed with regret that so few of Gainsborough's letters have survived, since the charm of his style is so fresh; it is easy to sympathise with him writing about his professional commitment to portraiture, on behalf of two fine ladies, his daughters:

> I'm sick of Portraits and wish very much to take my viol-da-gamba and walk off to some sweet village, where I can paint landskips and enjoy the fag-end of life in quietness and ease. But these fine ladies and their tea-drinkings, husband-huntings, etc., etc., etc., will job me out of the last ten years, and I fear miss getting husbands too. But we can say nothing to these things you know Jackson, we must jog on and be content with the jingling of the bells, only d— it, I hate a dust, and kicking up a dust, and being confined in harness while others ride in the waggon, under cover, stretching their legs in the straw at ease, and gazing at green trees and blue skies without half my *Taste.*[12]

Artists on their travels sometimes write letters which are good value, whether in praise or censure of what they see. Lawrence, for example, was in Parma in 1820, in ecstasy over the work of Correggio:

> Four times I went on long visits to the St Jerome, his finest work.

> How beautiful, how devoid of everything like the handicraft of art it is – the largeness, and yet ingenuity of its effect – the purity of its colour – the truth, yet refinement and elegance of the action, particularly of the hands (in which he particularly excels); and then, a lesson to all high-minded slovens, the patient vigilance with which the whole is linked together, by touches, in some instances small almost as a miniature, but like the sparkling of water.[13]

Diaries are perhaps more often a vehicle for complaints. Here is an American artist writing about his dismay at the work he saw at Paris in 1831:

> Although I had been informed that the present French artists were low in merit, I did not expect to find them, with little exception, so totally devoid of it. I was disgusted in the beginning with their subjects. Battle, Murder, and Death, Venuses and Psyches, the bloody and voluptuous, are the things in which they seem to delight: and these are portrayed in a cold, hard, and often tawdry style, with an almost universal deficiency of chiaroscuro; the whole artificial, labored and theatrical.[14]

Thomas Cole was not a diarist on the scale or with the range of one of the French painters, surely respected even by him, Eugène Delacroix. Delacroix's journal is articulate, concerned with other arts as well as painting, besides containing much comment on contemporary life. A passage of analogies in painting and poetry comes from September 1847. 'I see in painters prose writers and poets. Rhyme, measure, and the turning of verses, which is indispensable and which gives them so much vigor, are analogous to the hidden symmetry, to the equilibrium at once wise and inspired, which governs the meeting or separation of lines and spaces, the echoes of color, etc.'[15] Poetic painting was Delacroix's preference, but 'David's picture of *Leonidas at Thermopolae* is masculine and vigorous prose, I admit'.[16] In another passage in 1853, this time about *The Bathers*, a painting by Courbet, he invokes the aesthetic standards of music. He did not like Courbet's subject. 'The commonness and the uselessness of the thought are abominable; and if only his idea, common and useless as it is, were clear . . . Oh, Rossini! Oh, Mozart! Oh, geniuses inspired in all the arts, who draw from things only such elements of them as are to be shown to the mind! What would you say before these pictures!'

Artists' writing on art can naturally be more practical or technical, even in defining their own aims. The virtue of artists' writings for the reader of criticism is that it can often serve as a touchstone for judging the worth of mediators, particularly those presenting views of what the artist intended; what the artist said may be more to the point.

SCULPTURAL MONOGRAPHS

Books about sculpture have problems all of their own. The first and most obvious difficulty is that a three-dimensional object cannot fit satisfactorily on to a flat page. Different views of a sculpture can be presented, but you cannot move round a sculpture except with a film camera. There is also the problem of settings. Some sculptures are designed for their sites, and the relationship between site and sculpture is difficult to capture in a book.

Sculpture parks are an enjoyable innovation of the late twentieth century, or perhaps it would be better to say a welcome adaptation of an existing practice. In the seventeenth century Louis XIV had a sculpture park at Versailles, but it surrounded his palace, and was more formally designed by Le Nôtre, who needed sculptures for the focal points of his avenues. Twentieth-century sculpture parks are less rigidly planned, and intended to accommodate sculpture by artists in many different styles. The site can be adapted to suit the sculpture, which has a dominant role, unlike sculpture destined for the decoration of palatial gardens. Commemorative figures in city squares, portrait busts, tomb or cemetery furniture have also been traditionally restricted by the terms of commissions.

A consequence of this tradition is that the sculptor's own personality may receive less prominence in a monograph than a painter's, as the effect of patronage given or withheld can be decisive in a sculptor's career. The other major role of the sculptor is in the service of religion, where a high degree of interplay between artist and patron is not necessarily so important, making the sculptor's situation into one which is more like the painter's.

Writing on Auguste Rodin can make the point. According to George Heard Hamilton, Rodin became 'a figure of international significance, the most admired, prolific, and influential sculptor since Bernini'.[17] His secretary, the poet Rainer Maria Rilke, wrote with feeling about his work, but during the 1920s Rodin was less regarded, and not until after the Second World War did his reputation revive under the stimulus of exhibitions and increasingly careful cataloguing of his work. A decline of the sculptor's reputation derived not only from the political discredit into which the regimes of the years before 1914 had fallen, but also from a distaste for allegory, and a revulsion from naturalist sculpture (which the young Brancusi expressed forcefully as a dislike for 'beefsteak'). With the rise of modernism, Rodin's reputation fell; with the decline of modernism, Rodin's fame is growing again.

Rodin was a skilful salesman of his work, making careful use of photography in establishing and maintaining his good name. After 1900, he insisted that no photography of his work was allowed without his permission. There was a healthy demand for prints and postcards, which added to his income from the arrangements he had with photographers and agencies. As Albert Elsen has noted:

> We know that with major sculptures such as *The Burghers of Calais* and the *Balzac*, Rodin did not claim that they were equally successful from all points of view. He believed that these monuments succeeded compositionally from five or six angles. Given Rodin's collaboration with his photographers, these old photographs go far in answering the question from which points of view and from what distances they should be seen.[18]

What was true of Rodin's sculpture is also worth consideration by any reader of a sculptural monograph.

Another aspect of the matter is the question of scale. Reproduced to a uniform size on the printed page, sculptures which are monumental in size cannot be distinguished from those which are mere studies or maquettes. There is the possibility of misinterpretation by the reader. Some compensation may exist in sketches and preliminary drawings, where they exist, and which are easier to study on a page. These may take either the form of related drawings, or in Rodin's case, a free style of drawing which demonstrates his power of vivid creative improvisation with the human figure.

A further issue is how well sculptures are suited to their sites. Sculptural monographs often contain little information on this topic, and photographs of sculptures *in situ* are missing. Further, public response to works in prominent positions is rarely commented on. Yet for a work in a public square this is an interesting aspect of art criticism.

Perhaps in the last decade of this century something of a change in attitude to sculpture is becoming evident. The spaces in a city are more valued, and their enhancing is more a matter of public concern. Sculptures in cities are a part of cultural history, and can be the symbols by which the cities are known or remembered. Rome is distinguished by the statue on the Capitoline Hill of Marcus Aurelius; New York, even the United States, is symbolised by the Statue of Liberty; Copenhagen is remembered for its mermaid.

Also, the history of sculpture includes some account of the abortive plans for sculpture, just as the history of architecture is incomplete as a history of ideas without a knowledge of rejected proposals. Even though the same might be argued for painting, the technical obstacles to be overcome for painting are very much less than for sculpture. Again, this is where sculpture is closely alligned to social and political history.

MONOGRAPHS ON INDIVIDUAL WORKS

An art monograph need not be about a person, but can be about an individual work or a scheme such as a mural decoration. This is a fine opportunity for a sustained piece of writing, calling on a range of historical and artistic data, and including the art critical views not only of the author, but also criticism written at other periods.

A recent monograph of Jacob Epstein's memorial sculpture to the naturalist W. H. Hudson at Hyde Park Corner may be used as an example. Terry Friedman's book contains fourteen chapters, which chart the development of the work and its public reception – a stormy one. The topics include the first design, the sculptor's aims, the carving of the work, the memorial's defenders and attackers, and a final general reflection on the standing of great art and how it is likely to provoke opposition. The monograph is accompanied by a facsimile of a sketchbook for the memorial, and documented by letters and printed sources, including articles in the press. The art criticism of the day is fully described in the monograph, and some of the underlying reasons for its mainly aggressive character are outlined; these include anti-Semitism and the fierce dislike of the monument by some academic sculptors. A guide to London public sculpture described the monument as 'A masterpiece by the much-advertised apostle of Ugliness',[19] a view shared by those who felt that Hudson the nature lover was ill commemorated by a sculpture which showed nature in so raw a state. Comparisons of the sculpture with other contemporary works are included, and a summary conclusion implies the eventual security of the controversial sculpture in its Hyde Park home.

The Hudson memorial is not widely known, but the scope of this monograph is exemplary. Similar treatment can be found in works on great monuments and schemes, perhaps especially in the Italian Renaissance, when such projects as the Sistine Chapel or Tintoretto's Scuola di San Rocco achieved a personal artistic unity of the highest standard. For art historians, incomplete schemes or dismembered works such as altarpieces have the attraction of needing detective work; but a critic takes an interest in a reconstruction only if it throws new light on surviving art.

The main strength of this sort of monograph is its potential for detailed interpretation. As a book on a single subject, there is a good chance that the need for description will be reduced by extensive illustration, while a favourable judgement on the work has already been implied by the choice of the subject for a monograph. The interpretation of imagery, the circumstances of production, the place of the work in the artist's career, the historical context, the precise information about the work's appearance and condition, these are things that can be fully discussed in a monograph.

VERSATILE ARTISTS

A monograph on an artist who practises in several fields can be unusually interesting, since the writer's brief is to write with equal competence on different topics. Occasionally the challenge is too daunting, and teams of writers combine forces rather than one author attempting to rival the knowledge and skills of a Leonardo. More frequently work in different media is split up into specialist studies, so that although there are general studies of Gauguin's work, there are also specialist monographs on his prints, and on his sculpture and ceramics.

The versatile artist raises the question of relationship between the arts, and how far they can be considered to have the same or similar aims. In the nineteenth century it was Richard Wagner whose extraordinary ambition it was to make a complete artistic environment, in which the arts would blend. Historians can point to the philosophical views which underlay this ambition, and artists and sculptors were in various ways affected by the demonstration of its realisation in the theatre built for the composer at Bayreuth. The collaboration of artists with the stage was also brought to a high point by Serge Diaghilev, in his commissions to artists for the Russian Ballet. This connection between painting and the theatre was important to earlier European art in religious as well as secular performances.

Critics no less than artists have wide interests in the arts, and may introduce comparisons in their interpretations. In the nineteenth century to say that a picture was poetic was a common term of praise. In the present century emphasis on formal qualities in the visual arts have made musical comparisons more frequent, emphasised by the use by artists of musical terminology, as when Kandinsky chose to call his works Improvisations and Compositions. According to this formalist approach art aspires to the condition of music, a phrase employed by Pater, but deriving from classical Greece.

Clearly artists working in several media have a wide range of references. The art critic is thus bound to consider with care what standards of comparison should be used. In the late twentieth century artists working in performance pose difficulties for the critic, though some observers find it refreshing rather than troublesome to consider work beyond the easel picture and the individual sculpture.

In sum, then, the monograph is a major site for art critical writing, and, moreover, the place where the most extended criticism is likely to appear. The reader may be disappointed by the standard of what is written, but unlike other sites of criticism, this cannot be attributed to the form of publication, only to the limitations of the author. In a monograph, the author has the best chance of a free hand.

5

Panning angles: the catalogues

CATALOGUES RAISONNÉS

The second half of the nineteenth century saw new standards achieved in art historical scholarship, both through the careful study of documents and by close scrutiny of works of art. The results of these studies were published extensively in catalogues of private and public collections, and in what in French are termed *catalogues raisonnés*, that is to say complete lists of artists' works. Such catalogues were important to scholarship and also to the art market. If a scholar authenticated a work as by a major artist, then its price was certain to be higher.

A hero of this period was Giovanni Morelli, a remarkable Italian connoisseur who started publishing essays on pictures in public collections in 1874. His decisive opinions about the correct attributions of authorship in pictures were founded on a personal method, partly inspired by his medical training. He paid close attention to characteristics in a painting so apparently insignificant as the shape of a nostril or the lobe of an ear, arguing that such details were too unimportant for a follower to copy exactly. For example, Morelli wrote: 'In all those works by Raphael in which the *execution is entirely his own*, the ear, like the hand, is always characteristic, and differs in form from the ears of Timoteo Viti, Perugino, Pinturicchio, and others.'[1]

Typically, Morelli participated in one of the Swiss glacial expeditions organised by Louis Agassiz. Agassiz later became the foremost zoological teacher in the United States, basing his teaching practice on the observation of nature. Agassiz discouraged the use of books, except for research work. One story about his teaching is that a new student would be told to observe a fish in a tank. After some time the student would return to report. 'Look again,' he would be told. After a week, Agassiz's object lesson in respect for examining nature had made its impact. Morelli's insistence on observation was a comparable approach to learning.[2]

Morelli's method was extended by other scholars, and joined to systematic examination of documents. One of Morelli's youthful students was Bernard Berenson, whom Morelli described in 1890 as 'an extraordinarily scholarly young man who had already advanced far in the study of art'.[3] The young Berenson was a polymath, whose brilliant career at Harvard led his friends to pay for him to visit Europe to continue his studies. It was in Berlin that he first read Morelli's work. Four years after their meeting he published an account of Venetian painters of the Renaissance, where he acknowledged 'his indebtedness to the first systematic writers on Italian painting no less than to the perfectors of the new critical method, now adopted by nearly all serious students of Italian art'.[4]

Berenson had found his vocation: 'to be sure that every Lotto is a Lotto, every Cariani a Cariani, every Santecroce a Santacroce'.[5] His book on Lorenzo Lotto, published in 1895, was subtitled 'An Essay in Constructive Art Criticism'. He spent the rest of his life in expertise, painstakingly cataloguing the pictures and drawings of his favoured period, the Italian Renaissance, and in giving advice, notably to the great Bostonian collector, Mrs Gardner, and the main dealer of the period, Joseph Duveen. Berenson's decisions on attributions are listed in a reference catalogue, *The Italian Paintings of the Renaissance*.

The Morellian method had opponents, among them some of the German scholars of whom Morelli made fun by his articles. His judgements were impressive nevertheless, so that some critics were reduced to agreeing with his conclusions while denying the validity of his system. Before his day, and after it, there were scholars who relied more on intuition. Max Friedländer, an outstanding scholar of Northern European art, took the view that accepting a work into an artist's oeuvre was like recognising a friend, not a matter of measurement or detailed scrutiny. The reader is thus relying on Friedländer's eye. A difference between Morelli and Friedländer is that the former explains his method, while the latter does not.

More than a hundred years have passed since Morelli started writing; in that time many problems of authorship have been solved, while about others tacit agreement has been reached. The results of this process can be read in detail in catalogues raisonnés, which often give a blow-by-blow account of the arguments of scholars over the years. Here is a summary account of Manet's favourite painting by Tintoretto, the self-portrait in the Louvre. It comes from a book on Tintoretto by Hans Tietze (the references are left out).

> On the engraving of the picture made by Gisbert van Geen in 1588, for which Pozzoferrato supplied the ornamental framework and

> which Ridolfi reproduced in his biography, Tintoretto is described as being seventy years old. According to this the picture must have been painted about 1588, with which the style and the age of the sitter agree. From a letter to Francesco Gonzaga, written in 1622 and published by A. Luzio, in which among others a self-portrait of Tintoretto is offered to him, Pittalunga argues that the Paris picture may have been the one mentioned and which formed part of Rubens's estate.[6]

This sort of reading is only for the dedicated follower of the history of taste, though any reader particularly interested in a picture may find within a single catalogue entry an acutely discriminating judgement or interesting facts; for example, Tietze's entry also points out that Manet so much admired the Tintoretto self-portrait that he made a copy of it.

The catalogue raisonné continues to be a key document for authentication of an artist's work. As the decades have gone by, scholarly work has piled up, so that this category of book has taken a larger, longer and much more expensive form than before. Today catalogues raisonnés are often divided into two; one volume is for an introduction and plates, while the other has the detailed catalogue. Disputes over authorship are fiercely fought, and in the nature of things, frequently impossible to resolve with finality. However, the reputation of the cataloguer may be in some instances considered decisive; the picture is by Van Gogh if it is in the book by de la Faille; a painting by Berthe Morisot needs to be approved by Bataille and Wildenstein; an authentic work by Picasso will be found in Zervos.

Problems of authenticity are not so great for modern art as for other periods, even if a gifted forger like the painter Elmir de Horty can fool some of the people for some of the time. Catalogues raisonnés of modern artists do not depend on scholarly guesswork at attributions, and thus lack the laconic critical judgements reached by connoisseurs. In compensation, pictures or sculptures may be accompanied by comments from the artists. Additionally, the cataloguer will be sure to make comparisons, which will be useful to the reader, for the format is one of the few in which a generous number of illustrations can be included.

Any compiler of a catalogue raisonné will have seen and compared all the works listed, or will scruple to state if some work has proved inaccessible. At this level of personal and intimate experience there is little competition from other observers; only a handful of people in the world will ever see all the works in a catalogue raisonné. The scholar who completes such a work thus has an edge on other writers, so a preface can be read with the respect due to a first-hand account of the works concerned and a considered piece of reflective criticism.

EXHIBITION CATALOGUES

Exhibitions are major arenas for spectators of art, as well as for artists' struggles to achieve reputations and recognition. This section will consider not what the critics write in reviews of exhibitions, but the criticism which is contained within the exhibition catalogues; not the commentary from the box, but the programme of events.

A first broad division between types of exhibitions needs to be made. There are shows which could be grouped under the heading of historical exhibitions; there are mixed exhibitions and group exhibitions of works by living artists; and there are exhibitions in dealers' galleries, notably solo shows. The catalogues which accompany these events have rather different characters, for although there are entries for the exhibited works in each sort of catalogue, and usually an introduction, historical catalogues often have additional essays. Catalogues of major shows have also become bigger and more expensive in recent years, usually through the help of national, industrial or commercial sponsorship.

A characteristic historical exhibition may be called something like 'The Age of Rembrandt', or 'Shock of Recognition; the landscape of English Romanticism and the Dutch seventeenth-century school'; both of these are actual titles. Such catalogues include accounts of relevant historical research, and may cause new original historical work to be done. Individual works may be studied more carefully for a catalogue entry than ever before. In several ways, then, a catalogue may be in advance of any other publications. The corollary is that some catalogue information has only a limited life, since it may in its turn be overtaken by new research.

In the introduction or other essays there may be some writing which will not date, such as art criticism which documents the personal experience of the writer. Take, for example, this record of a personal response to Picasso's sculpture *The Man with a Sheep* by the critic Tim Hilton in the catalogue for 'Picasso's Picassos' in 1981:

> *The Man with a Sheep* is said to be humanitarian; that is far from one's experience in front of it, and the assertion is not much supported by the iconographical evidence. Is this a king who is the shepherd of his people? Or a priest of some unknown religion who strides towards us, implacably set on some atavistic rite? In the drawings the lamb appears to have bound feet, and the purport of the piece is surely more to do with sacrifice than deliverance.[7]

Some art criticism in a catalogue may be included so as to document the history of taste. For example, in 'The Shock of Recognition' John Constable's love for the work of van Ruisdael is highlit. Another entry, for

The Ancient Oak by Jan van Goyen (painted in 1642) seeks to explain a later English attitude to a seventeenth-century work:

> The ancient, weathered oak is the main motif, a theme as much used and loved by the Romantic poets and painters as the old willow tree. The execution, however, and this is typical of the 17th century Dutch masters, is more minute; and the composition, completely determined by a diagonal, is stricter than that of the English painters. According to 18th century principles the painting is 'sublime' in the roughness and irregularity of the tree, as well as 'beautiful' in the smoothness of the water.[8]

An instructive and recent example of a historical exhibition is 'Making Their Mark', toured in the United States during 1989. The subtitle of the show was 'Women artists move into the mainstream, 1970–1985'. The catalogue is 300 pages long with eight essays, as well as artists' biographies. In this instance the individual exhibited items are unnumbered and put in a check list; the main critical writing is within 136 pages, written in ten sections by Judith E. Stein (six sections) and Ann-Sargent Wooster (four sections on video). Such a catalogue inevitably tends to describe and characterise artists rather than evaluate them, while interpretation is likely to be left to quotations from the artists. Here is a passage about a picture by Judy Rifka: 'In *Square Dress*, a dancer, seen from above, is set off against an exuberant field of abstract color patches and architecturally evocative lines and circles. Segments of the athletic composition push forward into the viewer's space because Rifka has affixed additional forms onto the surface plane.'[9]

Elsewhere, Thomas McEvilley writes: 'One day in 1970 fifty thousand women marched down Fifth Avenue in New York. It is said to have been the biggest women's gathering since suffrage days, a little more than half a century before . . . H. W. Janson's *History of Art*, the standard college textbook, did not at that time mention a single woman artist';[10] and in discussing the period reviewed by the exhibition, various choices of media made by women artists are chronicled, for, 'Many women artists eschewed painting – especially abstract painting – as a domain polluted by long saturation with male dominant values, and developed their themes in performance.' On the central issue raised by the subtitle of the show, art in or out of the mainstream, some statistical study was made of the representation of women artists and the milestones in their careers. The catalogue as a whole is thus a document in the history of taste, a historical account, and at the same time contains some art criticism, not always explicit in evaluating the works shown.

'Making Their Mark' could equally well have been called a mixed exhibition; but this is a term more often used for a show put on by an exhibiting society, that type of artists' organisation whose importance in Europe was created by the middle classes, who sought in the eighteenth century to buy pictures rather than give commissions, as aristocratic patrons had been accustomed to do. Mixed exhibitions tend to have rather perfunctory introductions and catalogue entries; the same is often true of exhibitions arranged by groups of artists, though they may have statements of aim or even an artists' manifesto. Generally, art criticism connected with mixed and group exhibitions is commentary from outside, so that we shall return to them, with only this brief mention here, in the next chapter.

We can consider solo exhibitions instead, in either public or commercial galleries. Major art museums may devote considerable resources to an individual artist's exhibition, on the same scale as a historical show. But one feature of a catalogue of an exhibition for a living artist which is different is the likely inclusion of reminiscences from colleagues and members of the artist's family, who may make enlightening comments.

A dealer will have chosen his critic with special care for an introduction, an ideal candidate often being a sympathetic friend, perhaps a curator. In 1904 Sidney Colvin was Keeper of Prints and Drawings at the British Museum. Colvin had known Burne-Jones, and was persuaded to write a preface for a London gallery show. His text preserves a careful balance between deference, quotation and his own selective critical comment:

> The nature of Burne-Jones's aims and predilections in art are well-enough known by this time, and have been defined by himself absolutely fitted to this thought: 'I mean by a picture a beautiful romantic dream of something that never was, never will be – in a light better than any light that ever shone – in a land no one can define or remember, only desire.' If any one element in his style is to be singled out as predominant, it is that haunting expression of far-away desire never absent from the eyes and lips, and conveyed in every gesture, feature and attitude.[11]

Giacometti was an artist with very different artistic aims, clearly expounded by Valerie J. Fletcher in a catalogue for an exhibition at the Hirshhorn Museum and Sculpture Garden, Washington, in 1988. Writing about a small bust on a column, a thin sculpture in a series of four busts of which the others were fuller in form, she comments that 'the extremely thin proportions of the head contrast with the solidity of the base. So delicately modulated are the forms of the head that the human element appears ephemeral. This tenuous fragility contrasts with the three later busts on a stele, which have substantial anatomical forms.'[12] The sculptor had decided that he wanted this bust to confront the observer. 'In these sculptures I tried to make an eye. I raised the head on a base until the eye

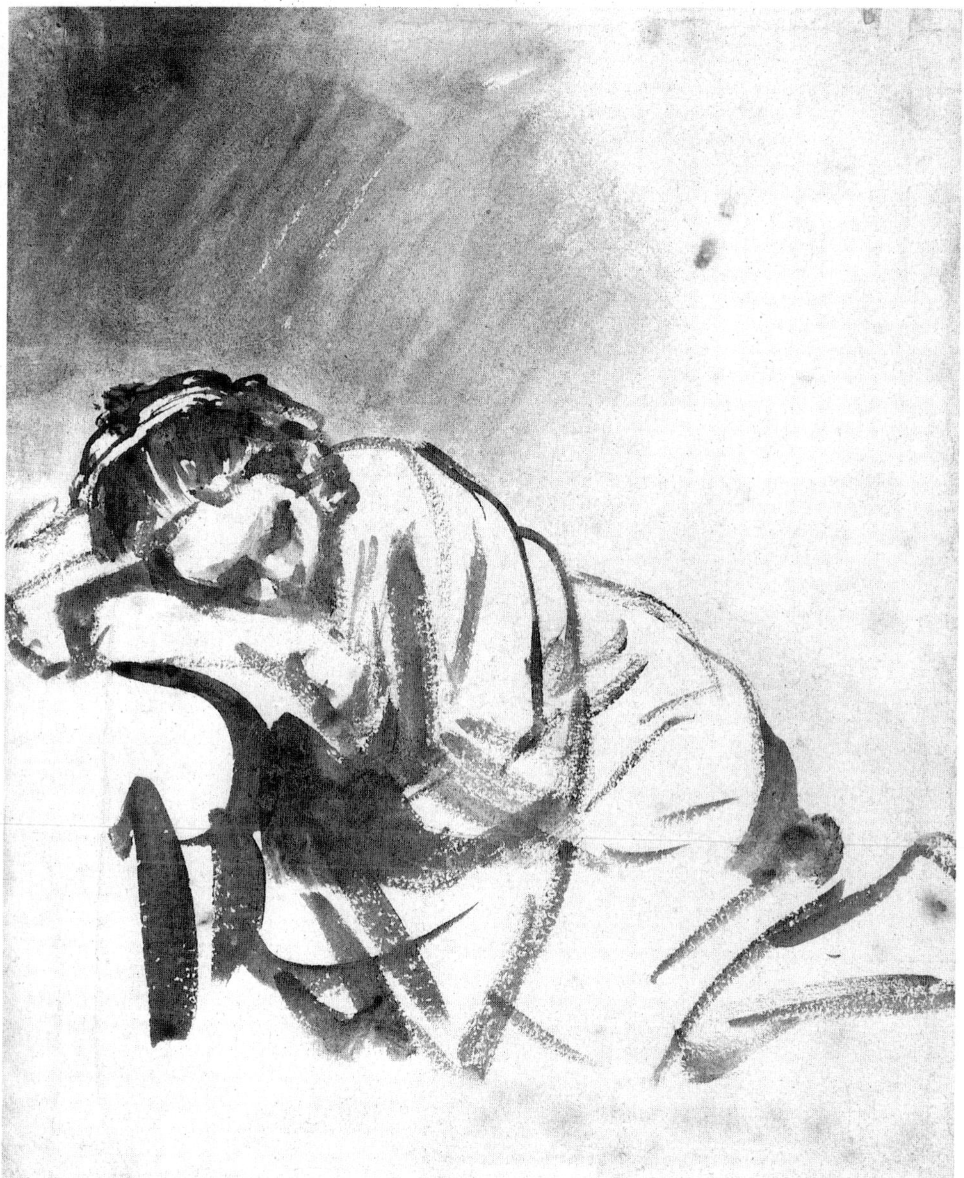

1 Rembrandt *A girl sleeping*

This is the first of sixteen illustrations in the section. They document the appearance of works of art of different sizes and in different materials with varying degrees of inadequacy. See also Wind's comments (p. 30), and the list of illustrations.

DESCRIPTION This is not a girl. This is a reproduction of black and white photograph of a brush drawing in bistre on a piece of paper, 30.3 cm high and 24.5 cm wide.

INTERPRETATION The subject is believed by some scholars to be Rembrandt's second wife, Hendrijcke. The drawing is generally agreed to be by Rembrandt, and is dated by Otto Benesch in his six-volume catalogue of Rembrandt drawings as in the middle of the artist's career.

EVALUATION According to Benesch, 'The present drawing represents a culminating point in grandeur and mastery of drawing with the brush'.

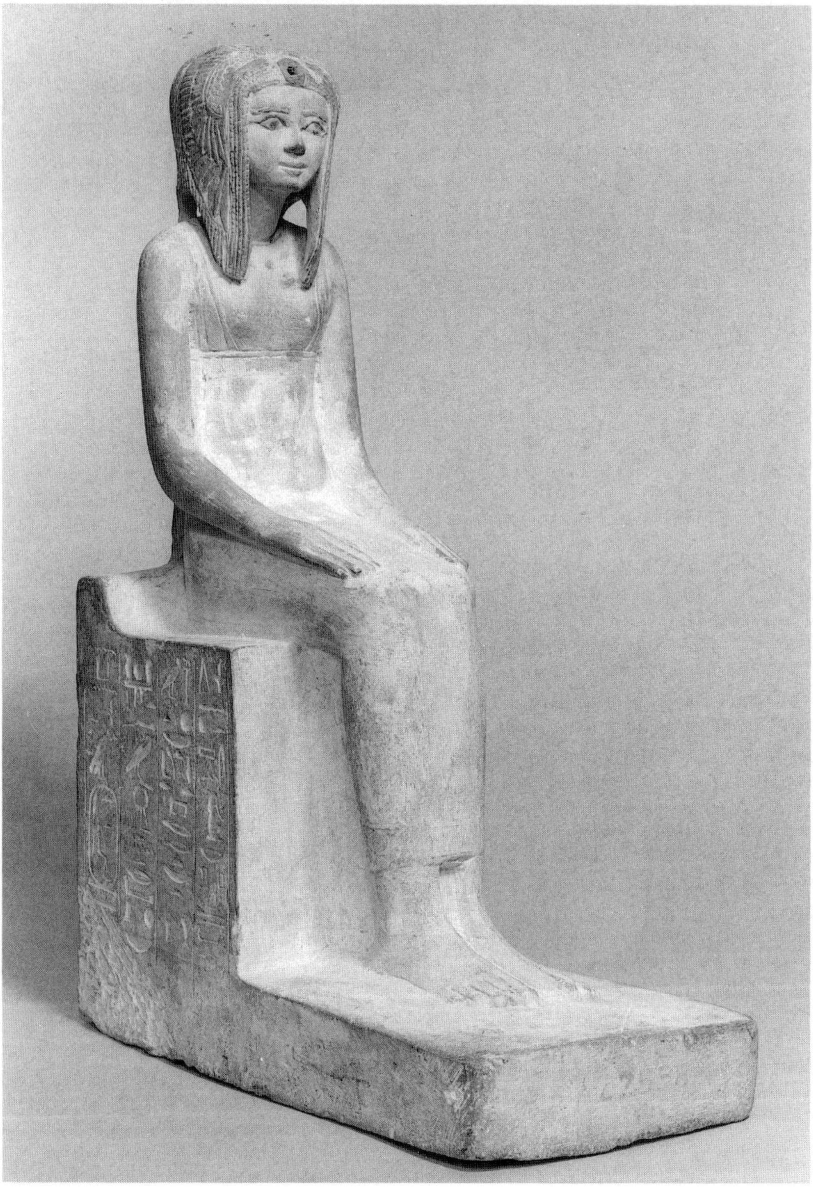

II Egyptian culture? *Queen Teshiteri*

Like the fraudulent Greek bronze horse in the Metropolitan Museum, New York (see p. 65), this work was long considered a key piece in the study of a culture. The limestone carving is 36.5 cm high.

DESCRIPTION Close observation has revealed elementary errors in the carving of the hieroglyphs, and oddities in the style of the figure.

EVALUATION The carving is now believed to be a forgery, made in Egypt shortly before 1890, not a genuine work of Queen Tesheriti's period (around 1550 BC).

This sculpture and the following item were featured in the exhibition 'Fake' at the British Museum in 1990.

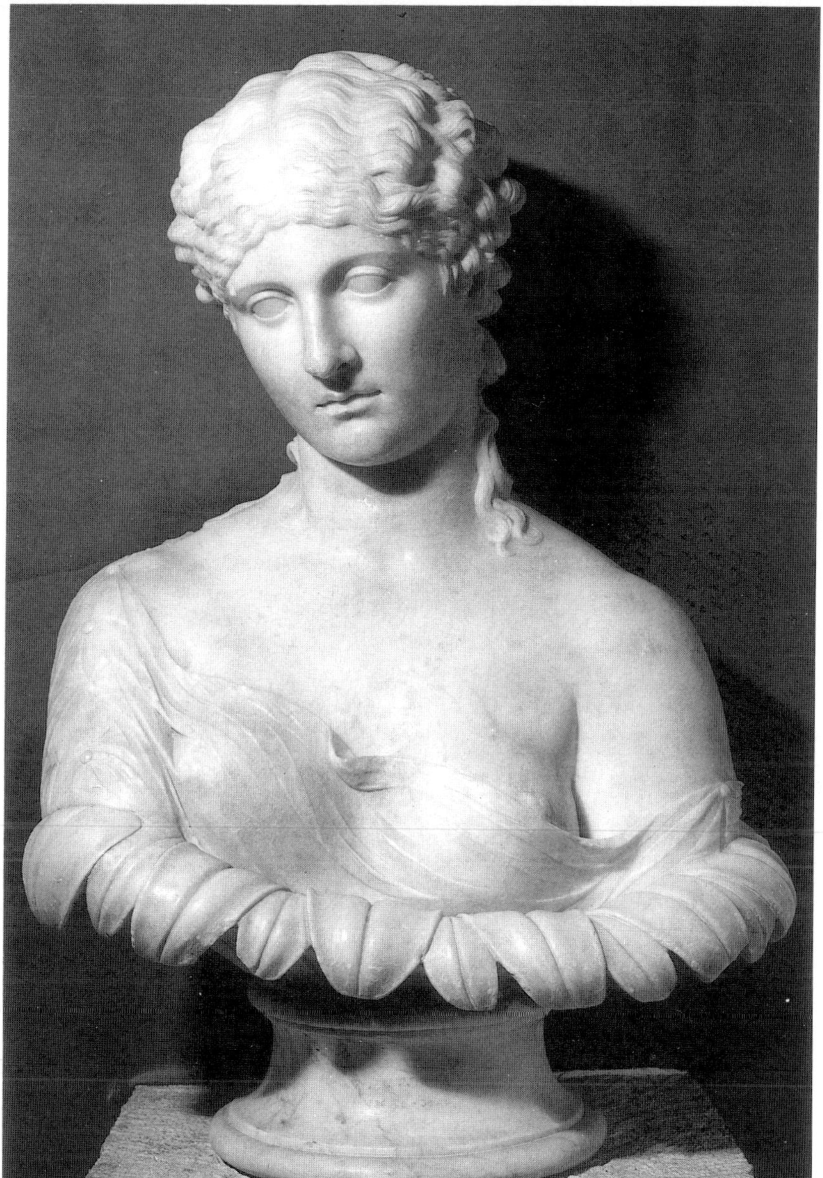

III **Roman culture, probably recut** ***Antonia?***

DESCRIPTION This marble bust, 57 cm high, appears to have been recut.
INTERPRETATION It may have been carved around AD 40–50, and altered in the eighteenth century, but some scholars believe it is from the latter period. If the bust represents a Roman sitter, she may be Antonia, daughter of Mark Anthony, and mother of the Emperor Claudius. In the eighteenth century the bust was known as Clytie, a nymph turned into a flower for the unrequited love of Helios, the sun god.
EVALUATION Technical evidence does not resolve the issues. Here is an excellent example of evaluation depending on interpretation.

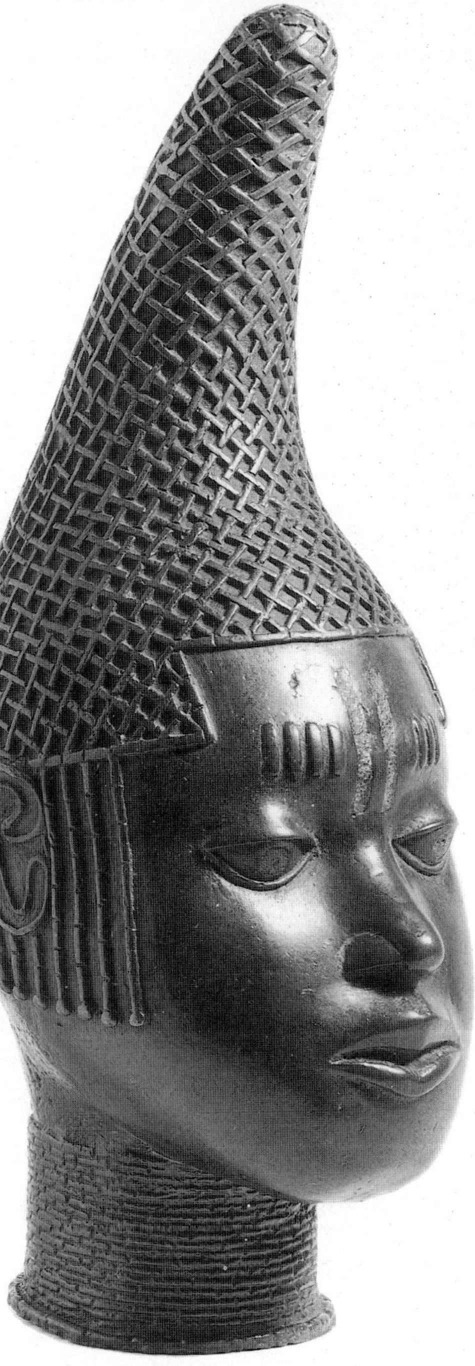

IV **Benin culture** ***A Queen Mother***

DESCRIPTION This brass head is 39 cm high.
INTERPRETATION Neither the sculptor nor the date of the head is known. Comparisons suggest it was as court commission made within the period AD 1100 to AD 1600.
EVALUATION The representational style, and the familiarity of examples in public collections since the turn of the century (see p. 105) make the work easier for a Westerner to enjoy. Other African sculptures, whose forms used are inventive and symbolic, can be more difficult.

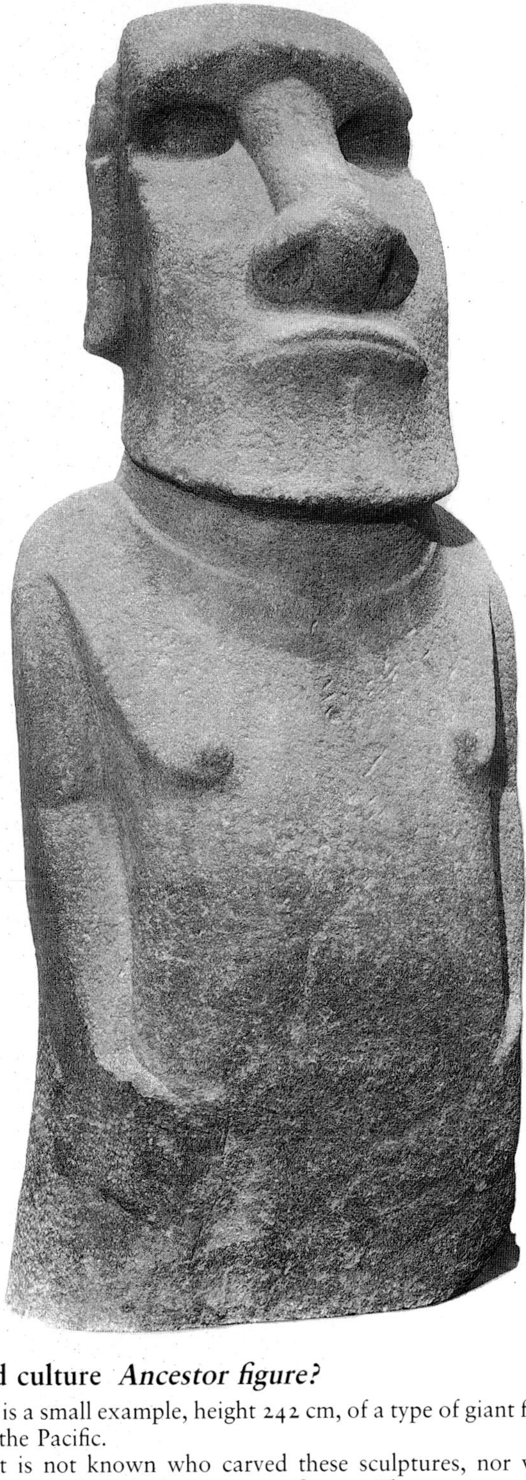

V Easter Island culture *Ancestor figure?*

DESCRIPTION This is a small example, height 242 cm, of a type of giant figure found exclusively on Easter Island in the Pacific.

INTERPRETATION It is not known who carved these sculptures, nor when, nor is it certain whether they are correctly described as ancestor figures. They are presumed to be the work of an extinct culture, for when Easter Island was first visited by European ships, the visitors found these figures were not standing, but fallen.

EVALUATION This figure is less impressive out of context. Many scultpures *in situ* have now been placed upright. Their strong but enigmatic presences have become famous through photographic reproductions.

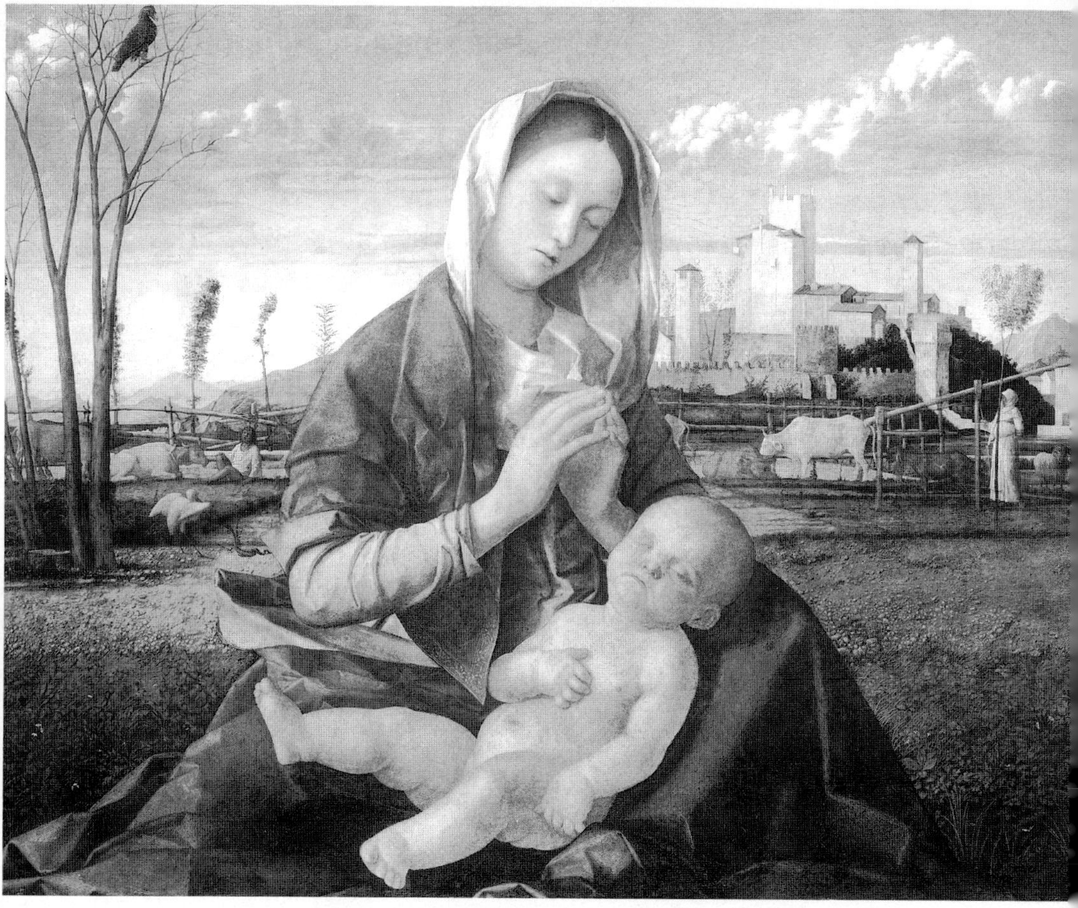

VI Bellini *Madonna of the Meadow*

DESCRIPTION The condition of this painting, 67 cm high and 86 cm wide, is not excellent; but the Christian theme of Virgin and Child is enhanced by a North Italian landscape setting.
INTERPRETATION Scholars have wavered about the picture's authorship (for the difficulties of Bellini scholarship see p. 64).
EVALUATION In 1901 a National Gallery handbook made the following comparison; 'A very charming little picture, marred only by a certain insipidity in the expression of the Madonna . . . which contrasts markedly with the pathetic type of Bellini's early Madonnas, and with the more stately type which he afterwards adopted'.

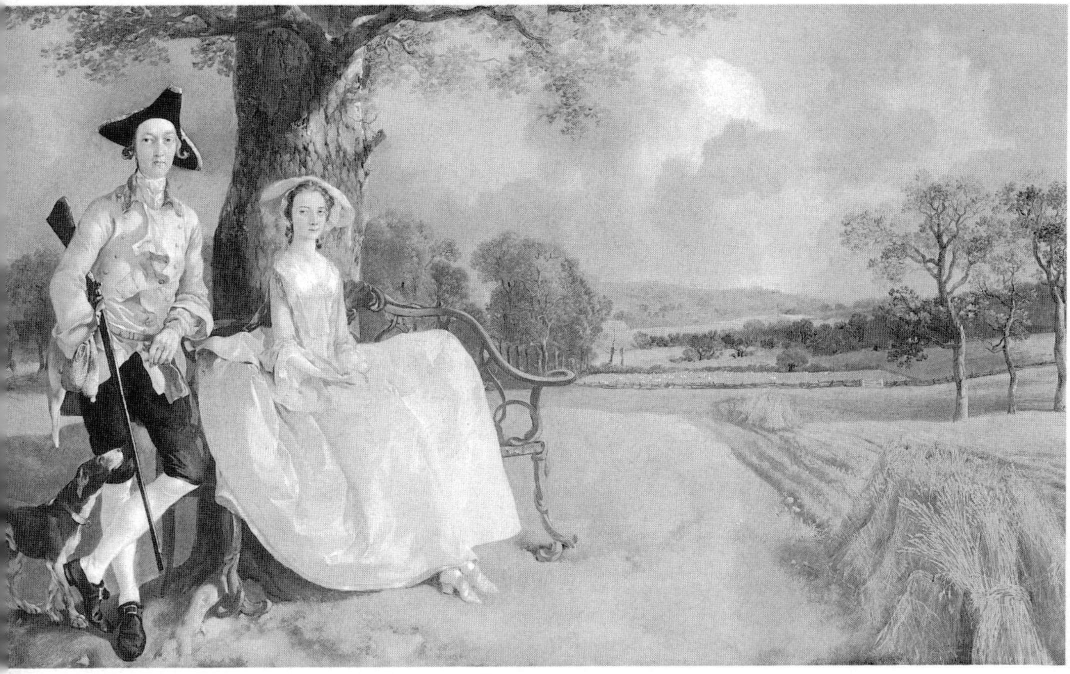

VII Gainsborough *Mr and Mrs Andrews*

DESCRIPTION The happy pair are in fine clothes, standing by a tree in front of a well-ordered agricultural landscape.
INTERPRETATION This delightful scene has become a battlefield for critics; some interpret the subject as the couple enjoying natural beauty, while others see landowners exulting in their possession of profitable farming land.
EVALUATION This is a lucid and frank painting, typical of Gainsborough's early work, and in contrast to the different and more feathery technique that he later adopted. As in other cases, critics decide on what terms of reference to use.

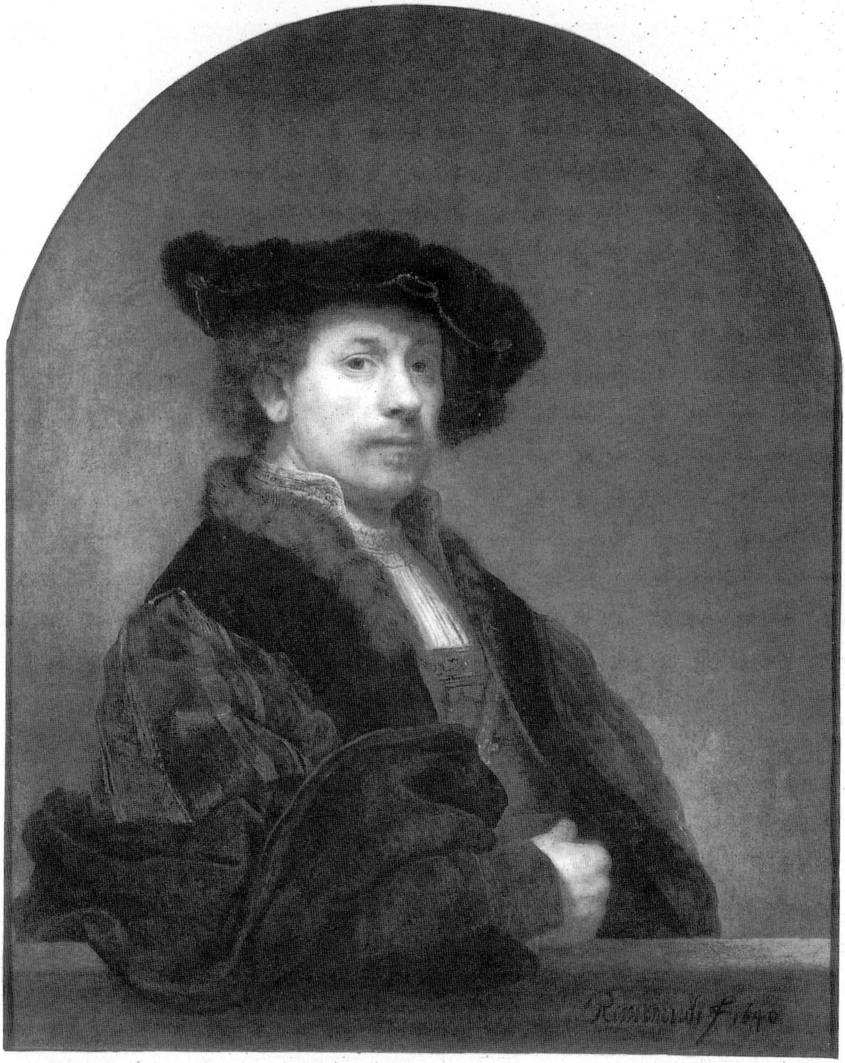

VIII **Rembrandt** ***Self Portrait***

DESCRIPTION This portrait (102 cm by 80 cm) is dated 1640, when the artist was thirty-four during a period of high reputation and prosperity. This is reflected in his costume. The head is minutely finished; the colours in the picture are rich but sombre, centred on browns.

INTERPRETATION There is no shortage of interpretations, which range freely through speculations about Rembrandt's character, art and career. Scholars have pointed out that the pose echoes portraits by Raphael and Titian.

EVALUATION The handling of the head is unlike later broadly painted self portraits, which some critics see as more deeply revealing, perhaps because of the sad circumstances of the end of his life. Praise is rather more muted about this painting of a successful professional artist.

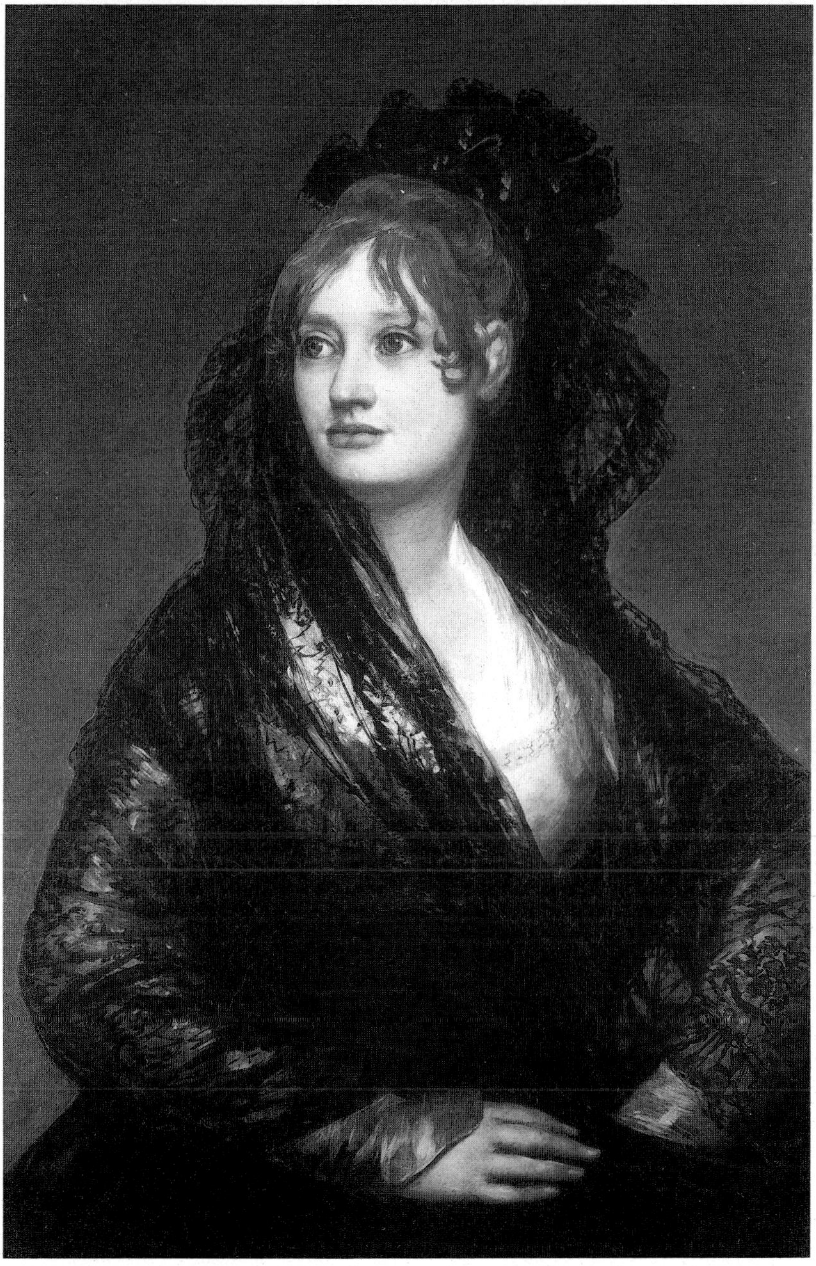

IX Goya *Isabel de Porcel*

DESCRIPTION This portrait (82 cm by 54.6 cm) is in good condition, the painting of the face being highly finished. The tonal contrasts in the picture are strong; reproduction in black and white gives satisfactory information about this tonal range, but obviously not about the delicate flesh tints. The sitter is wearing 'maya', an adaptation of gypsy costume, fashionable in Spain in the early 1800s.

INTERPRETATION The painting is in a special category of images, since it is seen as characteristically Spanish, just as Constable's *Haywain* is thought to be essentially English. Such charismatic images are difficult to see as works of art distinct from their embodiment of national sentiment.

EVALUATION The immediate attraction of the portrait can be measured against other portraits and in the wider context of Goya's work (compare pp. 102–4).

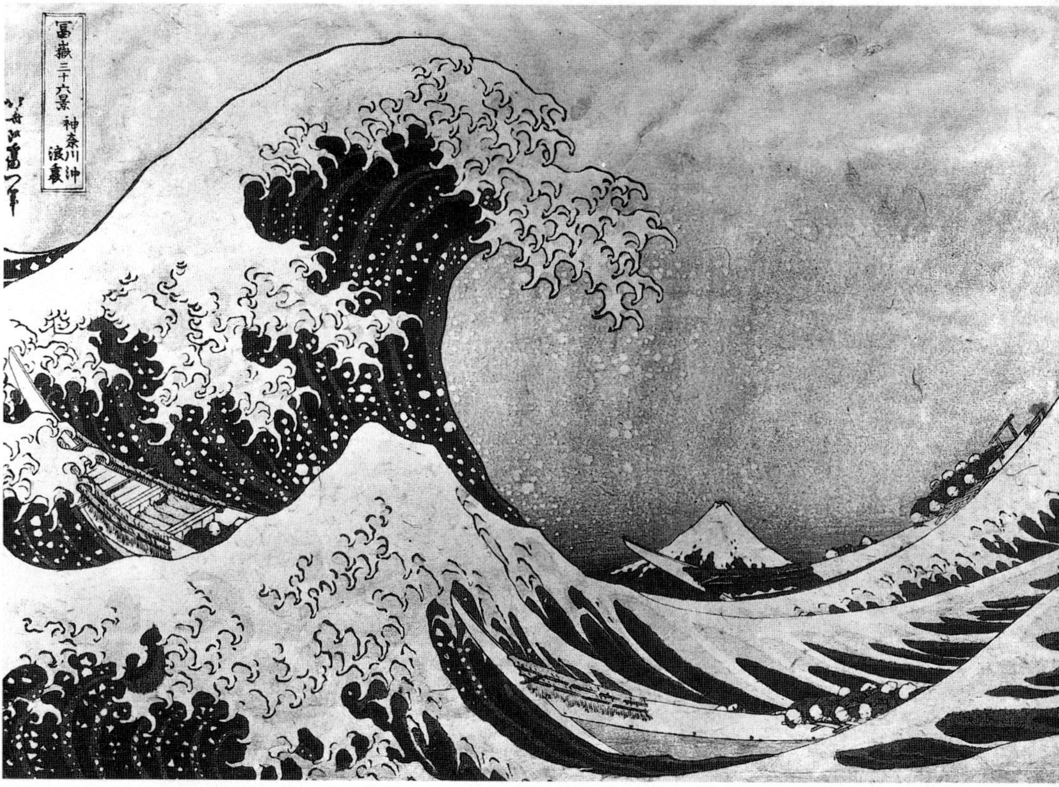

X Hokusai *The Wave*

DESCRIPTION This woodblock print (25.5 cm by 38 cm) is an exceptional design on the theme of views of Mount Fuji. The mountain is dwarfed in the distance, and a viewer has to look carefully for the three cargo boats caught in the storm, and search out the people on board. The predominant colours in the print are blue, while white is used both for the crests of the waves and the snow on the mountain.

INTERPRETATION The image is one of thirty-six views in the series which Hokusai carried out in the 1830s. The dramatic composition draws on Western perspective, while the theme contrasts the power of nature with human frailty. Musicians may remember that it inspired Debussy to write *La Mer* in 1905.

EVALUATION This masterpiece is one of the most highly esteemed prints of the series, though some connoisseurs prefer the simple but beautiful *Red Fuji*.

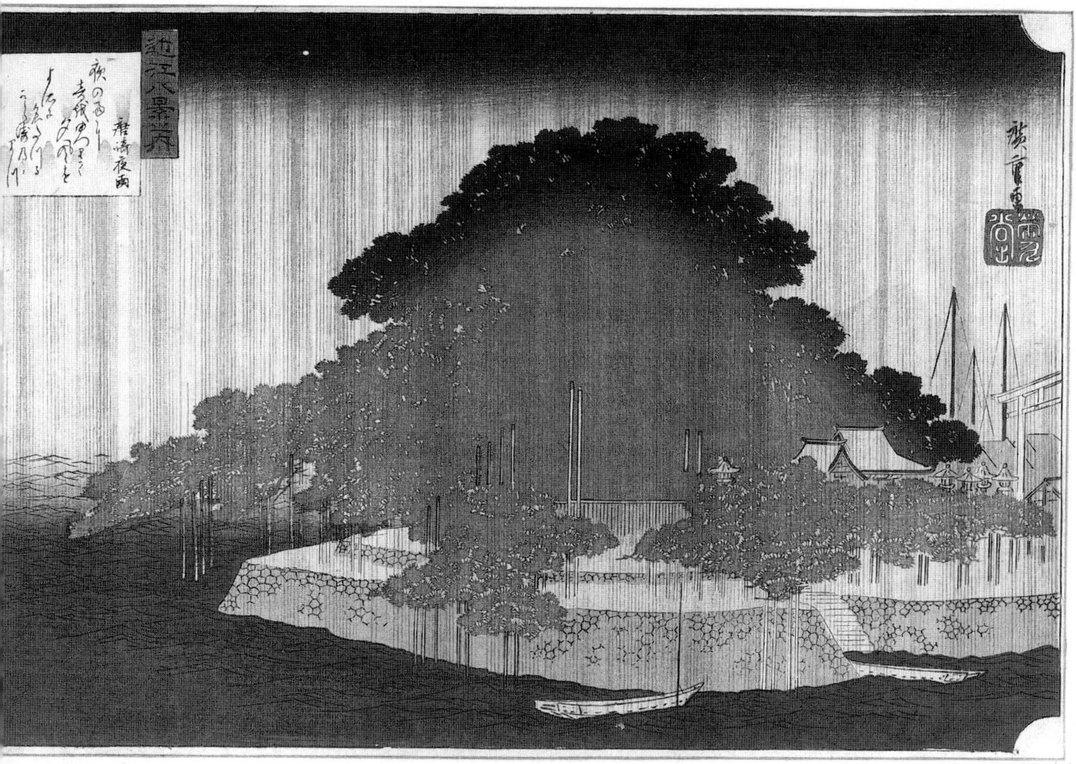

XI **Hiroshige** ***Night rain at Karasaki***

DESCRIPTION Hiroshige's woodblock print (25.5 cm by 38 cm) of Karasaki shows a venerable pine tree, supported by stilts, which shelters a shrine. The main colours are shades of blue and black, nuanced by different proportions of the colours in individual examples.

INTERPRETATION This is one of eight views of Lake Biwa. The scene is identified with classical Chinese poetry.

EVALUATION Richard Lane gives the following judgement: 'As with much of Hiroshige's most appealing work, it is the more spectacular forces of nature – snow, mist, rain, dusk, moonlight – that lend the final enchantment to a graceful composition anchored in a bedrock of natural quietude'.

XII Albers *Departing Yellow*

DESCRIPTION This square picture (76.2 cm) in which three yellow squares are superimposed is one of several studies for *Homage to a Square*.

INTERPRETATION The catalogue entry states; 'Most importantly Albers was able to invest and maintain vitality in his design by his deliberate device of symmetry in appearance but in fact only on the vertical axis. As he explained "This semi-concentric figuration avoids completely four-sided symmetry which would result in static fixation . . ." In words and work he reiterated: "We do not see colors as they really are. In perception they alter one another".'

EVALUATION The cataloguer sums up: 'In Albers' eye and hand seemingly mechanical and fixed laws become agents in creating allusive and mutable meditations on art'.

XIII **Rothko** ***Light Red over Black***

DESCRIPTION The reproduction is not helpful to a reader trying to make an evaluation. The presence of this large work (232.5 cm by 152 cm) is impossible to reproduce, and is notably incomplete without its colours.
INTERPRETATION The artist's single idea, wrote Rosenberg, was like a sonnet or a Japanese poetic form, the *haiku* (see p. 71).
EVALUATION Maquet wrote an approachable sort of criticism about a work by Rothko by describing his responses (see p. 91).

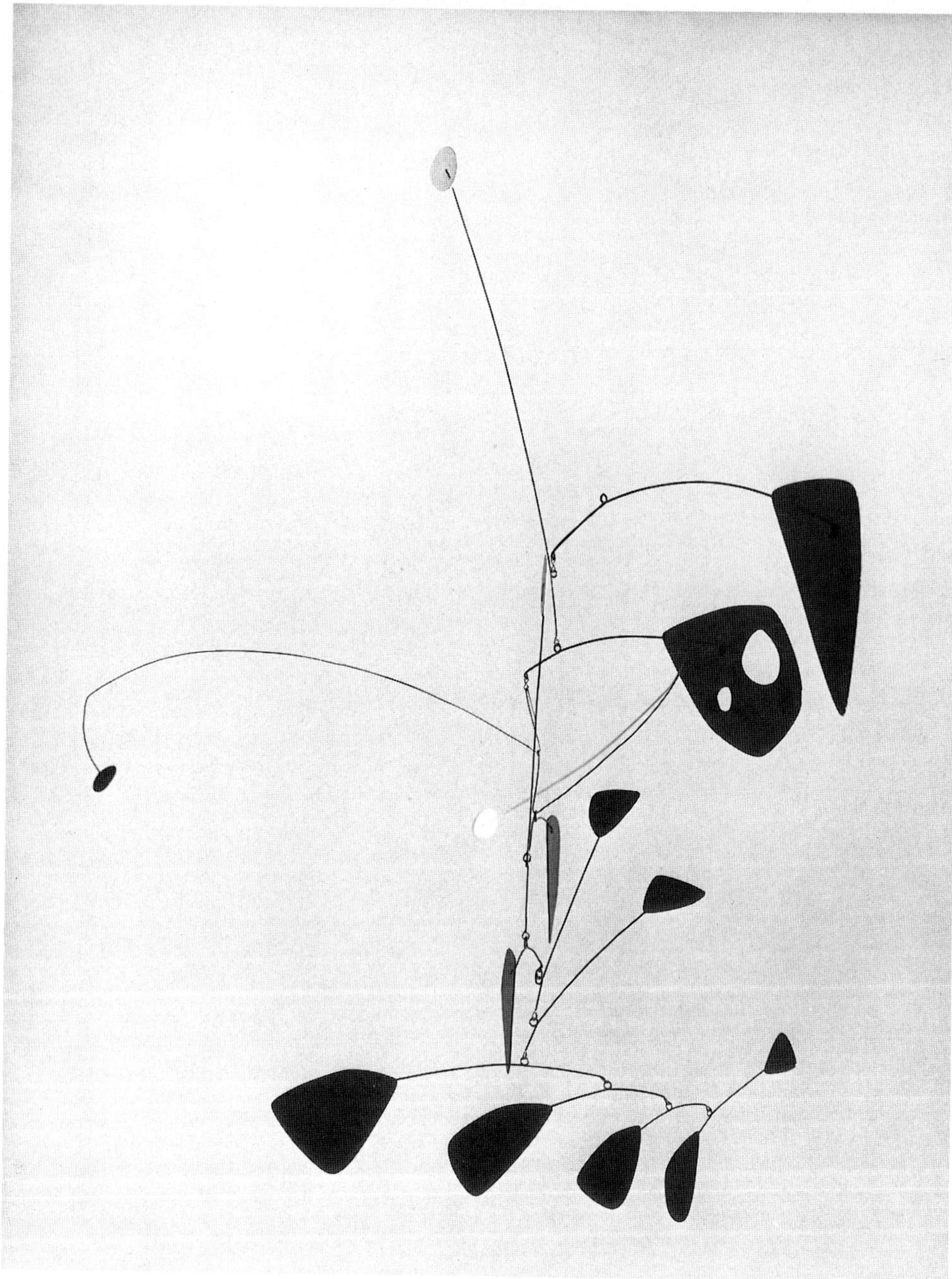

XIV Calder *Mobile*

DESCRIPTION This work, made of sheet aluminium and steel wire, hangs down 111 cm, while its maximum extension is 128.2 cm. It is called *Antennae with Red and Blue Dots*, and its different parts move in currents of air.

INTERPRETATION A mobile sculpture is obviously fun; but interpreters have picked out Calder's affinities with his contemporaries like Miro, and the connections of his work with sympathetic source material in weathervanes and hanging shop signs, circuses or folk arts.

EVALUATION This has not been easy, as some critics have felt that such entertaining art should be demoted to a low category, or perhaps does not even qualify as art. In the past, hierarchies of subjects, listed by academies or in catalogues of collections, have provoked similar misgivings (see p. 39).

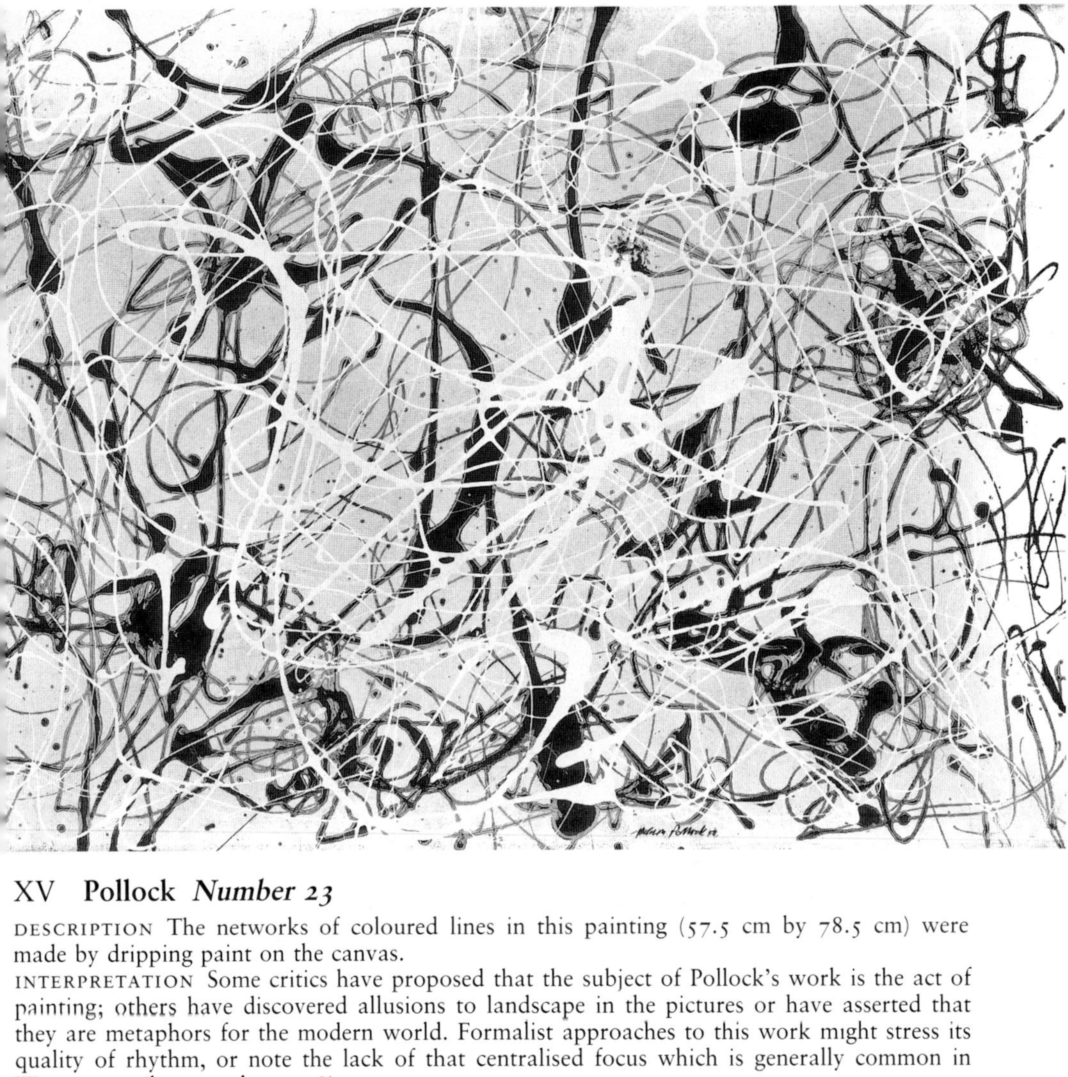

XV Pollock *Number 23*

DESCRIPTION The networks of coloured lines in this painting (57.5 cm by 78.5 cm) were made by dripping paint on the canvas.

INTERPRETATION Some critics have proposed that the subject of Pollock's work is the act of painting; others have discovered allusions to landscape in the pictures or have asserted that they are metaphors for the modern world. Formalist approaches to this work might stress its quality of rhythm, or note the lack of that centralised focus which is generally common in Western art (but see also p. 98).

EVALUATION Another instance of evaluations being closely connected with interpretations.

XVI Kelly ***Broadway***

This last image is a provocation, since it is virtually impossible to use alone for description, interpretation or evaluation.

A critic commenting on Ellsworth Kelly's work is likely to make comparisons with examples from his other periods, thus interpreting this work in a sequence of development.

The very limited description which would be of some interest in this case is the colour (red) about which the reproduction gives no information.

This image may also be considered as a last caution against expecting too much from reproductions.

is at eye level. You see an eye.' This intention differed from the sculptor's frequent artistic aim to make his small figures appear remote.

The catalogue has the additional interest of a memoir by Silvio Berthoud, who had sat as a boy between five and eight for his uncle:

> I have very unpleasant recollections of sitting for him, for it was of utmost importance not to move but to fix him right in the eye and listen to him complain, saying as he always did that he was getting nowhere. It was not much fun, particularly at my age . . . Things would deteriorate rather quickly, for Alberto would return to his hotel in the evening with a sculpture eight to twelve inches tall under his arm and come back the next day with a piece no more than three or four inches high . . . I later realized that I had posed during a crucial period, and the tiny bronzes that resulted (for that size prevailed) continue daily to touch me. [13]

Another example from the 1980s allows us to hear a conversation between the critic Norbert Lynton and the painter Ken Kiff.

> Kiff set out to make an image of a man writing. Mayakovsky's poem 'An Amazing Adventure of Vladimir Mayakovsky' surfaced as he worked. It celebrates creativity amid doubt and despondency – creativity as energy but also as a duty, work to be done by man as it is the sun's task to shine. I have pointed out to him that his picture echoes the medieval and Renaissance formula for St John on Patmos writing the Book of Revelation and for the evangelists writing the Gospels, itself derived from Greco-Roman author portraits. This was not his intention but iconographical echoes of this sort do not surprise him.[14]

The writer goes on to make further points about the picture's elements.

These examples of catalogues containing helpful art criticism could be contrasted with many others which are limited to lists of exhibitions, details of the artist's career, and entries for the works displayed.

There are other hazards for the readers of catalogues. Some publications are less impartial than they might appear, erring on the side of generosity. Museums with exhibitions of art from other countries are especially likely to be respectful in commentaries on works of art which have been borrowed. All the same, museum curators will have carried out a critical task in selecting the exhibition, in some instances having fended off proposals for inclusions with a political or a particular cultural bias.

In a commercial gallery, the size of the rooms is decisive. It might make artistic sense for the gallery to borrow some key picture to enhance the look of an exhibition, but a picture which is not for sale is an expensive use of wall space. Finally, it is safe to predict that in any catalogue there will be more information than art criticism.

AUCTION CATALOGUES

Buying and selling art is at its most dramatic in an auction, a fact that auction houses are quick to exploit. In the last three decades there has been considerable success for auctioneering, both in terms of money and also in prestige. The idea that a price at auction is a definitive market price has even become quite generally accepted, although in fact auctions are subject to manipulation like other markets described by some economists as free.

An undeniable attraction of an auction is the possibility that some undervalued item may be for sale. The auction houses employ considerable skill to ensure that the best possible prices are obtained for their clients, but all the same, a good eye and a well-stocked memory may still outwit their expertise. An occasional exploit deservedly catches the newspaper headlines, like the case of a picture spotted by a London dealer, David Carritt. Sothebys were unfortunate enough to misattribute a French eighteenth-century picture, which was in fact by Fragonard. Carritt bought it, correctly identified it as a lost early work, and magnanimously sold it to the National Gallery, London, far below the market price.

Auction catalogues do not carry critical comments on individual items for sale, but there are sometimes introductions with criticism. An example is the catalogue of paintings by Noël Coward, which was prefaced by a memoir of the playwright, describing his interest in painting. In marketing a sale of rather little-known works, too, there may be some explanatory text. It would be wrong to dismiss this sort of criticism as mere sales talk, particularly in grand auctioneers' catalogues, though there is little danger of such publications being reticent. Part of the charm of a sale is that the financial result is in itself a sort of critical judgement, reflecting even if not defining the taste and mood of the moment. But an auction is mainly a bullish market; vendors are trying to improve their prices, and few except dealers are selling on the market's way down, in order to rebuy. This bearish tactic does not work as well as in a stock market, for art works are widely dispersed, and decisions to buy or sell may be thoroughly unpredictable. One view of the art market is that it is like a staircase with several landings. Only dealers sell on the steps, while private owners prefer the more certain floor of a landing of clearly established prices for a category of work.

Correct descriptions are important to auctioneers, as can be exemplified by the coding used to list paintings. This is the system used by Sothebys:

(a) references to signatures, inscription and dates refer to the present state of the work;

(b) the term 'bears a signature' and/or 'date' and/or 'inscription' means that in our opinion the artist's name and/or 'date' and/or inscription have been added by another hand;
(c) the term 'signed' and/or 'dated' and/or 'inscribed' means that in our opinion the signature and/or date and/or inscription are from the hand of the artist.

Such caution is prudent in a business where errors of judgement can be extremely expensive; at least the reader of an auction catalogue knows clearly what view has been taken by the cataloguer on a number of questions. The auction catalogue can also quote from other authorities, which will be inevitable in a case where a scholar has written a catalogue raisonné, and advantageous if the context of the work is made clearer by the artist's correspondence or other publications. Long catalogue entries recall the cynical remark that the price of a painting is in ratio to the length of the bibliography in the sale catalogue.

Besides seeking to establish the authenticity of works in the sale room, auctioneers are also concerned that the title to ownership is secure. The indirect evidence of critical approval by a succession of owners may be interesting to a reader, though admittedly this demands some special knowledge about the standing of the collectors concerned. Luckily for the curious, this historical sideline can be followed up in a number of publications, both about individuals and institutions.

The authentication of works of art from other parts of the world can be problematic. For African art, say, the difficulties are complicated by lack of written or other corroboration, and knowledge that extensive copying has been done. Thefts of art works are also an international problem, especially poignant in the case of objects with cultural and religious significance.

Occasionally auctions contain items so interesting that critics in newspapers comment on their quality, not just the prices they might fetch. More often auctions are not reviewed; this is a pity, since the management of markets in art deserves scrutiny. The visitor to an auction may be caught up in the excitement and drama of the event, but the climate of opinion in which it takes place has been created by scholars and critics as well as businessmen.

MUSEUM CATALOGUES

Casual visitors to art museums generally prefer short guides to the official catalogues. Some guides are indeed very brief, suggesting visits at breakneck speed where only a few items or rooms will be seen. Is it Tuesday between eleven o'clock and noon? This must be the Albertina.

A museum catalogue is an imposing task for a curator, so daunting indeed that some museums never publish one. Difficulties can be many, at the top of the list being the number of items to be catalogued. Happy indeed is the curator of a select collection like the Mauritzhuis in The Hague, where one collector's policy was to limit his collection to thirty excellent works, lesser works being discarded to make way for better. The curator's nightmare is somewhere like the Smithsonian Institution in Washington, where the number of items is like grains of sand on the sea shore.

A model for art museums is the catalogue of the National Gallery, London. Divided into national schools, in separate publications, the gallery also publishes short guides, souvenir guides, books of details, a complete photographic record of the pictures, specialist publications on conservation, and educational material. The keystone of the arch of publications must be the catalogue itself, from which the authority of other writing derives.

The catalogue of the earlier Italian schools was written by Martin Davies, and published in 1951. The strength of the gallery's holding of works by Giovanni Bellini made it worth the author's while to write a preliminary note about difficulties of attribution:

> A definition of Bellini's oeuvre is one of the hardest problems in the history of painting. The first difficulty is, despite the destructions, the enormous number of existing pictures, many of them signed, and in one way or another more or less Bellinesque. It is obvious that Bellini had assistants to help him in his studio; indeed, there is documentary proof of that. But the question of what pictures are entirely or for practical purposes Bellini's own is answered largely by personal taste; there is therefore a considerable divergence of view.[15]

The catalogue of the German school was published in 1959, and written by Michael Levey. The entry for number 291, a portrait of a woman, is a fair example of method: 'The quality of [the picture] seems sufficiently high for it to be acceptable as from Cranach's own hand. It is associated by Friedländer and Rosenberg with a group of similar female portraits, and shows clear analogies of handling.'[16] The connoisseurship demonstrated in these two examples is built up from an accumulation of work by many scholars, but in the end, the cataloguer has to make a judgement, which for number 291 is in favour of Cranach's authorship.

Sometimes subjects require considerable explanation or interpretation, and in these cases the museum catalogue can give definitive help. Interpretation of iconography, the historical context of works, or personal information about sitters for portraits are only a few of the varied topics which can be spelt out in catalogues. The level of detail may seem much the same as in a catalogue raisonné, but the stress falls in a different way. In a catalogue raisonné an individual work is related primarily to other works by the artist, while a museum catalogue entry will extend to other contextual information and comparisons.

Some of the work for a museum catalogue may have already been done before the acquisition of a picture. It may, for example, have been part of a private collection which itself was catalogued, especially if the collector in question was rich. In this respect, the scholarly standard of a private collection's catalogue will be very high, and the sort of information which a reader can expect will be the same. The collection will not, however, be accessible as public collections are. In an art museum works can be studied at leisure, and will receive attention from scholars and experts of many kinds. Besides, works can gain by the company they keep in a museum collection, a landscape being in a group of works of similar date and intentions, or a portrait seen among contemporaries.

One of the important features of museum collections is the function they have as touchstones of quality and authenticity. Paradoxically, it is in museums that the market in art is defined, since permanent collections place limits on what is available for collectors to purchase. Further, on the basis of knowledge about museum collections, artists can find help in choosing ways of developing the art of the present.

The museum is also the place where the closest consideration can be given to the troublesome problems of fakes and other forms of inauthenticity. Museums are at an advantage in making close examination of works in their own collections showing evidence about a picture, say, which can only be discovered by the newest scientific and technological methods. A critic walking for the first time into a gallery may describe a colour in a picture as blue; it will have been the scrupulous task of a conservator to have established that the particular colour in question was Prussian blue, and thus cannot date before the eighteenth century.

Old-fashioned amateurs used to admire colours with a golden glow, which conservators have demonstrated were the effect of discoloured varnish. The shape of a picture may have been altered, and the museum, though not a stray visitor, will know the fact. In short the pictures in an art museum have been closely monitored, often through decades and in a few cases for centuries, so full descriptions that appear in the catalogues have a thorough-paced authority.

It is also through observation that fakes are unmasked. Some have been living for a disconcertingly long time in museums; but once doubted, the evidence of inadequacy in a fake is quite often soon in coming. The Metropolitan Museum in New York, for example, proudly owned an early Greek bronze horse, which a sharp-eyed administrator on the staff noticed one day had a ridge. This vital fact proved its method of manufacture did not correspond to its supposed date. The museum made the best of a bad job. Joseph Noble, the observant administrator, announced to an audience of eight hundred, 'It's famous, but it's a fraud.'[17] More than that, it was 'one of the most important classical art forgeries ever discovered'. Some museums have prudently kept a collection of mistaken purchases, and even bought some forgeries deliberately.

CRITICAL PATHS

A climate of artistic opinion is as tricky to predict as the English weather, and also quite as changeable. Both writers and readers are affected by generally accepted ideas, without necessarily having given them independent thought. One difficulty in describing a climate of opinion is this fact: that many shared views are not stated openly, but assumed. A set of assumptions may be challenged by an outsider, and at this moment these shared views come into focus. To look at the work of an art critic in this way we have to turn to historians of taste for the past and to journalists for the present. When we do this, we find that a critic's range of activities varies from place to place and period to period.

Let us look at the second half of the twentieth century. In Paris art critics are often directly associated with particular galleries, and exhibition reviews may be negotiated for a fee between a magazine or a newspaper and the artist's representative. In London historians and critics are solicited for opinions by the auction houses, sometimes but not always accepting a fee; commissions for articles are independent decisions by editors. In New York, gifts of pictures by artists to critics may follow a favourable review, though a critic is likely to refuse payment, even for a catalogue introduction, from a dealer. The variations and exceptions to these brief generalised statements can be found in a number of books, some by investigative outsiders, some in memoirs by dealers and others interested in the market. For other periods, historians are slowly making studies which document the connections of critics and historians with the markets.

In 1959 Dore Ashton was dismissed by the *New York Times*, the charges being that her articles were not aimed at a wide newspaper audience, and her articles on work by artist friends gave evidence of bias (her husband, whose work she was forbidden to review, was a painter and print-maker called Adja Yunkers). John Canaday, the incoming editor of the newspaper's art page and responsible for the dismissal, had made a challenge to a climate of opinion in which Dore Ashton's criticism was valued for its sensitivity, and where the art which she praised was accepted. Her supporters included Thomas Hess, Meyer Schapiro, Leo Steinberg, Harold Rosenberg, and Peter Selz, and their intervention, asserting that Canaday had offended Ashton's 'rights and responsibilities as a critic', resulted in Canaday's being censured by the American art critics' association.

A case of unwitting collusion by a critic in a manoeuvre by an art dealer occurred in 1961, when Leo Steinberg wrote an article about Jasper Johns. Johns was a puzzling phenomenon for Steinberg, as one of the artists of Pop Art, then hardly begun. The article appeared in an Italian magazine *Metro*, who had intended to pay $300 for an article; but when Johns' dealer, Leo Castelli, knew that Steinberg was considering an article, he arranged for the magazine to offer $1,000, paying the difference of $700 himself. Steinberg knew nothing about it. The underlying question for a reader of criticism is what influences are exerted on the critic; but as in this instance, for long it may be impossible to know the truth.

One noticeable feature of American art life is the link between art historical teaching and criticism, not so common elsewhere. The practice of American art historians reviewing or curating exhibitions, not only historical shows, is a normal feature of art life. Part of the reason for this is that the American professoriat is the largest in the world, while the American market for current art is unprecedented; it is evident that the turnover of the American art market as a whole is the largest in the world. The persuasive tax advantages for the rich to contribute works of art to public collections also play a part, contributing a measure of prestige shared between artists and the powerful in society. Critics can also be invested with a degree of respect deriving partly from their academic connections.

Another sort of authority derives from money, which a reader of art criticism may find it difficult to dissociate from an object. Historical knowledge is the surest cure for this damaged intellectual condition, as the history of taste will show many examples of the irrelevance of monetary value to artistic quality. Incidentally, the good art critic should be the reader's friend in refusing to be impressed by art market prices. The English art critic Peter Fuller had an honourable record in this respect; despite Julian Schnabel's financial success, he refused to be intimidated by market values.

> Whatever flickerings of potential this young tyro possesses, they cannot cover up the fact that he is a painter with the imagination of a retarded adolescent; no technical mastery; no intuitive feeling for pictorial space; no sensitivity towards, or grasp of, tradition; and a colour sense rather less than that of Congo, the chimpanzee who was taught (among other things) a crude responsiveness to colour harmonies by Desmond Morris in the late 1950s. However, potentially educable as a painter Schnabel may or may not be, his work is just not worthy of serious attention by anyone with a developed taste in this particular art form.[18]

Readers need also to be wary of the existence of special markets. The explosive prices for Teddy Bears in the last few years indicate how a market can be created, in this case by a mix of merit and nostalgia. What is clearly a dealers' market is often signalled by the invention of a brand name to group together a variety of material, perhaps rather disparate. Pop Art is an example. Or a brand name may already exist ready for exploitation by a market-maker; Impressionism, for example, was ready to hand for British dealers to invent a new category of art which they could stretch to calling British Impressionism.

The influence of an international market is not easy to be precise about, though the appearance of work in a Biennale or an art fair can be impressive in itself. The critic here may be acting as an exhibition organiser or co-ordinator, critical decisions being mainly limited to selection.

Private collections are examples of critical judgement in action, so that both their catalogues and the opinions expressed by collectors are worth consideration. The collector may have pronounced views. Albert Barnes, the rich American industrialist who formed an outstanding collection between the wars, certainly promoted his personal theories. Barnes possessed excellent paintings by Cézanne. In a combative book, *The Art of Cézanne*, he expounded a theory of rhythm in art which he advanced as the key to Cézanne's success. Barnes wrote on scientific principles, he said. Here is a passage:

> The rhythmic movement of volumes and planes in space is so basic in Cézanne's design that it usually extends to the treatment of the background – whether that be sky, wall or drapery – and makes it serve the dual purpose of a screenlike area or space boundary and of a rhythmic sequence of semivoluminous planes which continue the movement of the units in the middleground and foreground; this sequential ordering thus contributes to compositional unity in the widest sense as well as to the expressive movement of the total form.[19]

Another collector with a firm sense of the importance of the pictures he had bought was Douglas Cooper. He specialised in collecting the work of four artists he considered to be the true Cubists, Picasso, Braque, Leger and Gris. In 1971 he was asked to organise, at the Tate Gallery, an exhibition which he called *The Essential Cubism*. The catalogue amusingly contains some entries with such comments as 'Compare and contrast this painting with two works of the "analytical phase".'[20] It would be worth knowing how many exhibition visitors obeyed these examination instructions.

Finally, the critic may well face an issue of authenticity. Here is a description by a French expert of a visit to the painter and etcher, Dunoyer de Segonzac. The artist was shown a watercolour:

I don't know what to say. I painted this bit here several times over; that hill too. But there's a lack of unity. Is the thing a fake? I can't be sure. Perhaps I wasn't on form the day I painted it. The worrying thing is my signature, which is extremely hard to counterfeit. But this one looks impeccable. There's only one solution, and that is to destroy the picture. It's second rate, in any case [he added smiling], so the artistic loss to the world will be nil. As for the purchaser, tell him to come to my house and choose another picture – something that both he and I like.[21]

6

Snapshots: the articles

THE SOLO EXHIBITION

The acid test for art criticism is the solo exhibition. This is the occasion when a reader can visit the same show and make a personal assessment of how helpful the art critic has been. At its best, art criticism will enable the reader to enjoy or appreciate an exhibition better. This fuller appreciation may result from a short or a long article, even occasionally some unexpected insight or well-phrased judgement; but it will not come from a brief comment off the cuff, an item of gossip, or a mere listing. The only virtue of these latter newspaper techniques is to bring an event to the attention of a reader.

A solo exhibition can vary in scope from the minimum, that is to say a show of recent work, through a more extended selection to the apogee of a retrospective exhibition. We have already looked at writing in catalogues, and can now turn our attention to the critical responses which appear in articles. The scope or character of a piece of criticism is naturally related to the magazine or newspaper in which it appears, as we noticed in the case of Dore Ashton's dismissal from the *New York Times* because it was asserted that her work could not be understood by the paper's readers.

The first rule for a reader of articles is thus to find a sympathetic publication. Some trial and error should eliminate the laziest papers, whose critics do no more than pillage catalogue introductions, or even press releases. Some latitude can be allowed to serious critics who write for periodicals which go to press a long time before a show is on view; these critics will not be able to comment on how the exhibition actually looks, as their articles will have been written before the show's installation. They nevertheless will have seen some, perhaps all the works included, and can thus comment usefully on the artist's standing, aims and achievements.

The content of an article will tend to be determined by its length; no newspaper article is likely to be more than 1,000 words, which precludes any chance of detailed analysis. Indeed, an article at this length will frequently avoid mentioning any work of art by name, being limited instead to a generalised description of an artist's work. For example, this passage in an article on Giacometti by the American critic Hilton Kramer:

> Every mark of his pencil, every touch of his brush, every effort to shape a figure or a head from the scrutiny of the model who sat before him, was felt to be an 'impossible' assault on an objective guaranteed to elude his grasp . . . This 'difficulty' was the moral center of his art, the very fulcrum of his style. To it we owe that nervous, spidery line of the drawings – so quick, so attentive, yet so despairing – that alerts us to the elusiveness of the subject at the same time that it perseveres in the attempt to render it.[1]

The article, called 'Giacometti's moral heroism', is about a retrospective show of the sculptor's work ten years after his death; it does not include the name of any single work.

Or an article can be centred on a motif, as this passage about Rothko by Harold Rosenberg indicates:

> By 1950, Rothko had conceived his conclusive insigne of a disembodied absolute. This icon consisted of the rectangle of the canvas as a one-colour ground visible along the edge of – and occasionally through an opening between – three or four horizontal blocks of color with brushed surfaces and furry borders. For the next twenty years, Rothko's work consisted of reanimating this pattern with the substance of his emotional life. It was as if he had conceived a latter-day, visual version of the sonnet or the *haiku*. Except that (and this is decisive in regard to the situation of the one-idea painter) his format was private – almost, one might say, the framework of another self, or of himself in another form – and unavailable to others.[2]

A further way of treating an article about an exhibition is to make a comparison with another artist. The painter Patrick Heron wrote for the *New Statesman* in London in the 1950s, and used this technique for writing about Braque, whom he compared with Picasso. The quotation is from an article of 1954, at a time when Picasso's reputation was very high. Heron was anxious to point out Braque's qualities, so he trailed his coat openly.

> To suggest, as I do, that Georges Braque is the greatest living painter is to remind a contemporary audience, fed to satiety on brilliant innovation, frenzied novelty and every sort of spontaneous expression, that, after all, permanence, grandeur, deliberation, lucidity and calm are paramount virtues of the art of painting . . . The rival genius of Picasso has proved to the world that our age may be epitomized by works which [show] his unfailing sense of visual drama, his protean invention and his power of investing his creations with a hallucinatory poetry.[3]

Heron shows in his article a deep sympathy with Braque's work, which, incidentally, was a sort of painting he himself was seeking to practise at the time. He argued that Braque enhanced objects:

> He is infinitely kind to all the things that go into his pictures. Indeed, the kind of life which he bestows on his coffee-pot or coffee-grinder, his table, his chair and window, is just the sort of life we feel these things are really living! The personality with which Braque invests his jug is something that the jug possesses in its own right. In other words, Braque divines the essential spirit – one might almost call it the 'soul' – of each object that he paints. For this reason we have the feeling that a Braque jug is just as real and valid, just as much a distinct unity, as the jug that comes from the potter's wheel.

PERSONALITY PROFILES

A profile of the artist is another form in which to review an exhibition. When such an article rises above the level of a gossip column, the artist's profile can be a valuable format. One source of interest can be a description of where the interview has taken place, perhaps a studio, or maybe the artist's home. After the Second World War, for example, the photographer Alexander Liberman decided to visit the studios of artists who had contributed to a century of painting in France, painters and sculptors closely connected with the School of Paris. He commented on his project: 'The more I explored, the more I became absorbed with the mystery of the environment. Why should France have become the focal center of painting and sculpture at this particular time? What relationship exists between the painting and the vision of reality that the artist has before his eyes? At no time have I believed that environment is a complete explanation of art. I am sure, however, that it plays an important role.'[4]

The photographs were taken over a period of ten years, and eventually they were brought together in a book in 1960; ten of the book's essays originally appeared in *Vogue*, where the appealing mix of an artist's conversation along with Liberman's descriptions and commentary succeeded well. Here is one of the descriptions from the profile on Georges Braque:

> He insisted that I visit the church and marine cemetery at Varengeville. The small twelfth-century edifice, built right above the steep cliffs that dominate the northern beaches of France, and the cemetery with its hundred tombs and crosses are in harmony with Braque's colors. The church is gray; the cemetery crosses are of white marble. The stained-glass windows inside, and the black wrought iron and living or artificial flowers outside, contribute vivid accents. The steel-gray expanse of the northern pebbled beach, overcast with the shadows of the high cliffs, creates the dominant black of Braque's marines. I understood how much Braque had absorbed the countryside around him.[5]

The *New Yorker* has a good record of commissioning articles. Braque was profiled by Janet Flanner, who also wrote evocatively about Picasso and Matisse. Flanner is rather sparing about details of Picasso's personal life, knowing it to be so extensively documented. But her selected information has a welcome sharpness:

> Even the opening report of him comes from an unusual source – his own vivid memory of how he learned to walk. More than sixty years after the event, while watching a child of his own try out his first steps, he suddenly stated in reminiscence and satisfaction to his most intimate Spanish friend, 'I remember that I learned to walk by pushing a big tin box of sweet biscuits in front of me because I knew what was inside.' What must have distinguished him as being beyond normal was his unconventionally high state of consciousness.[6]

Magazine profiles may be carefully written and prepared, though their facts are unlikely to be as thoroughly checked as in books. Newspaper profiles are quite likely to be based on interviews, which have an immediate attraction, though a reader will naturally be wary about how accurately the interview may have been recorded. Even taped interviews can only be read with caution, since they may have been edited, and the reader will not be told how. Besides, it is an everyday experience that people are sometimes wrong in conversation, and may not remember events well. Where personal profiles have a strength, however, is in what the critic says about personal reactions to artist and work.

One incidental advantage of personality pieces is that the magazines in which they appear may be able to afford good-quality colour reproductions. Unluckily, this may be of little help to the reader if the pictures illustrated are used as mere decoration, and not the subject of critical discussion. This is as unsatisfactory as reading about a picture which is not illustrated.

The crux of a personality article is that it aims to satisfy a reader's curiosity. An editor's directions to the writer of an article may be to take a populist approach, suitable for a wide audience. The article written to this brief is likely to have an element of sensationalism; curiosity about sex or money may be deliberately aroused; conflicts in an artist's life are likely to be dramatised. An amusing parallel in the film business is an account given by the director Ken Russell of how he sold the idea of making a film about Tchaikowsky; he described it to his potential backers as the story of a homosexual who fell in love with a nymphomaniac. Similarly, the personal lives of artists may be believed by editors to sell more newspapers than reflective criticism.

GROUP SHOWS

Reviews of group shows make hard reading. The critic may choose to write about common features in the work of the artists exhibiting; this may lead to generalisations about the group which take little account of the individual qualities of the artists. Indeed, the assumption that they have characteristics in common may be mistaken or misleading. The alternative, of choosing between artists, is also hazardous, since it refutes the idea that they have a reason for exhibiting together, even if what the critic writes is favourable. A hostile article is even less likely to be satisfactory to a reader. There is no problem for an antagonistic critic to find incoherence and inconsistency in a group exhibition.

To begin with, the reasons for which artists show together are varied. An obvious reason is financial, since to share costs of a show is easier for the participants. Another financial incentive is that sales may be generated by the naming of a group. At the end of the twentieth century group exhibitions perhaps do not have the importance that they have had earlier in the century. There are many galleries through the world, and it is no longer so difficult for an artist to show work independently. Solo shows and mixed exhibitions are more common, with the group show playing a less important role in the market.

Artists who group together for financial reasons may choose a name which is no more explanatory than a number or numbers. Thus in London at different times there have been groups which have called themselves the *Society of Twelve*, the *Seven and Five*, and *One/Four*. It could be argued that these groups were formed as much for sociability as for making money, being made up of friends or acquaintances, but at any event their reasons fell short of promoting definite artistic programmes.

A word of caution is in order, though, about the names of exhibiting groups. Sometimes a number conceals a genuinely significant programme, such as the *Group of Seven* had in Canada. This distinguished alliance of landscape artists sought to invigorate their country's artistic life by bold treatment of wild Canadian subjects. Tom Taylor, mentor and leader, had died before the group had its first exhibition, but remains classed with his friends. They subsequently developed individual styles and separate interests, as is true of most groups of artists, but their initial appearance was defined by a programme.

Another sort of title for a group is exemplified by *Der Blaue Reiter* (The Blue Rider). Forty-three works by fourteen painters were shown in 1911 at the 'First Exhibition by the Editorial Board of *The Blue Rider*', the publication concerned being an almanac which appeared in 1912 with a drawing of a horseman by Kandinsky on the cover. The second exhibition included thirty-one artists. The main need of these artists was for good opportunities to exhibit their work; unlike the equally celebrated group *Die Brücke* (The Bridge) they did not work closely together. Nor did they plan portfolios of prints, as *Die Brücke* did; a practice, by the way, followed by a variety of artists' organisations including the Senefelder Group in England, which has sold its members' lithographs from the nineteenth century to the present day.

Impressionism is the most familiar group with an artistic programme in the nineteenth century. Several features of its history are worth notice. For one thing, the group did not choose the name, which came from a reviewer's description of a painting by Monet. Then, the artistic aims of members of the group were quite varied, and some personal animosities caused the alliance to break up. Further, the name was partly kept alive by dealing, primarily by the man most heavily committed, Durand-Ruel. What was perhaps most crucial to the success of Impressionism in financial terms was its modern stance, as closely identified with contemporary life at the turn of the century as Romanticism had been fifty years before. In artistic terms, this modern stance inevitably attracted competition. Seurat and his colleagues argued that Pointillism was a scientifically modern style, while the Symbolists asserted that spiritual values were preferable to artistic programmes of perception.

The unfavourable reception of Impressionism by the French critics is notorious; but Impressionism was not the only group to gain a name from a review – the Fauves and Cubism share this. From a critic's point of view, a label, whether ending in 'ism' or not, is convenient. The critic writing in a newspaper with very limited space needs such a label to give the reader a general idea of what is on display. Using such a shorthand description leaves space for other topics.

Another consequence of the labelling of Impressionism and other groups by critics was that some artists naturally decided that they themselves could do the same job better than the critics. In Western art there had been artistic programmes and manifestos before Impressionism, but in the twentieth century they proliferated. Part of the critic's task in the nineteenth century, as now, was to interpret art for the lay public; but what, artists asked themselves, if we interpreted our own work? From such a thought sprang statements of artistic aims and manifestos, some using the new device of naming a group with a progressive title, such as Futurism. De Stijl is an especially bold assertion of identity, the Dutch word for style implying that there is no other style worth considering.

The reader in this situation has a choice: the work in an exhibition can be measured against the artists' manifesto; or the critic's interpretation and assessment can be used. The critic necessarily has to take a manifesto into account. Indeed, there is an implicit struggle between critic and artist; an artist's manifesto can be seen as a deliberate attempt to pre-empt critical comment and evaluation.

One puzzling decision for a critic to make is to decide whether to isolate any one artist as the leading figure of the group. When this is done, there is a tendency for other artists to be compared with the leader to their disadvantage. It is a nice matter of judgement to decide how to treat the various personalities with justice. Sometimes the teacher is absent from the group, as Gustave Moreau was absent from the painting exhibited by the Fauves; or, like Tom Taylor of the *Group of Seven*, he may be dead. Only time and scholarship eventually sort out the various relationships of artists who worked together.

Artists can be at a disadvantage in group exhibitions as only a small part of their activity can be seen. A small gallery may have space to show work in only one medium; this may have a distorting effect on the activity of the group as a whole or of versatile individuals. It may also give a misleading impression: for example, the work of German Expressionist painters under the banner of the name *Die Brücke*, Kirchner, Nolde and Pechstein was affected by their practice as print-makers, where some motifs and treatment originated. A show of their painting tells only part of their story. The knowledge of a critic is useful here for filling in relevant background information. The critic is also likely to spot the gaps in a group show, when the best works are not being shown, say perhaps because they are in private collections.

The politicising of Western art gives the existence of a manifesto special relevance. If the aim of an exhibition is political, the evaluation of art on purely aesthetic grounds is possible, but considered an irrelevance by the exhibitors. In the longer term, it may be something aesthetic will be seen in what was intended as pure politics. The prime example is the Dada movement, whose nihilistic work is now admired for qualities of imagination. It was originally reviled, as the artists intended, for its rejection of conventional values of art and society.

MIXED EXHIBITIONS

Mixed exhibitions are ideal for spotting talent ahead of the market, as well as being a significant source of income for many artists. The most common sort of mixed exhibition is the exhibiting society, whose history is entwined with the development of art in Europe since the eighteenth century. The shows put on in Paris at the Salon, and in London at the Royal Academy, were a means of creating sales for artists at a turning point in the history of patronage; as there developed a middle-class market for literature, so there developed a comparable market for art.

Denis Diderot gained lasting fame as the energetic editor of the French *Encyclopaedia*, but he is also rightly celebrated as an art critic. It was in 1761 that he first wrote an account of one of the Salons, which was circulated with his other correspondence in the fashion of the time by his friend Grimm. Diderot's standards were those primarily of a moralist, questioning how morality might be fashioned through painting, but he was sensitive to artistic aims; his essay on painting was admired both by Goethe and Baudelaire. Here is a description by Diderot of a Russian country scene by Le Prince, from criticism of the Salon in 1767.

> An old man has been playing the guitar, but he has left off playing to listen to a young shepherd piping. The old man is sitting under a tree, and a young girl is near him; I think he is blind – at least, he ought to be. The youth is sitting at a little distance, his shepherd's pipe in his mouth; there is a charming simplicity in his dress and appearance; he has a fine head. The old man and the girl are listening attentively. On the right are some rocks, and at the foot of them the sheep are feeding. This picture goes straight to my heart; I should like to lean against that tree between the old man and the girl and listen while the youth played. And when he had left off playing I would go and sit by him, and a little later we would all lead the good old man to his cottage. A picture that affects one thus cannot be a bad picture. You may say that it is feeble in colour and monotonous in tone – it may be so, but it touches the heart, it arrests the attention; and what is the use of all your correct drawing and pure tints, and skill in light and shade, if your subject leaves me cold and unaffected. Painting is the art of reaching the soul through the eyes, but if the picture appeals to the eyes and never reaches the soul, the painter has fallen far short of his aim.[7]

In person, incidentally, Diderot was an encouraging critic. Sainte-Beuve tells us that David

> always spoke of Diderot with gratitude. It seems that David had at first great difficulty in making his way with the public, and was several times unsuccessful in his efforts after fame. It was at this time that Diderot, who often strolled into the artists' studios, paid a visit to David, and saw a picture which the artist was just finishing. He admired it and talked about the artist's meaning, and the noble ideas he attributed to him. David listened and frankly avowed that he had not been conscious of all these grand ideas. 'What,' said Diderot, 'you did it from instinct without knowing what you were doing! That is better still!' David was greatly encouraged by this warm admiration expressed by a celebrated man, and it helped to develop his talent.[8]

Reviews of exhibiting societies' shows have constantly presented difficulties to critics, as it is only possible to give brief comments on some of the artists' work; how could it be otherwise when an exhibiting society shows several thousand works? During the nineteenth century to be noticed was good fortune, while to be praised was a professional advantage.

Exhibiting societies, once established, bred rivals; the most remarkable rivalry in the nineteenth century was in Paris, where the choice of pictures for the Salon in 1866 was so generally considered to be unfair that the rejected pictures were shown in a Salon of their own. This enabled some major figures to show work for the first time. By the end of the century, a pattern emerged through Europe of societies of artists breaking away from official organisations, creating seceding groups, of which one in Austria adopted the word as a title, *Sezession*.

The problem of criticising the work in exhibiting societies' shows is how little space is made available in newspapers for its coverage; the critic has time to mention a painter or a sculptor, make a brief observation, and then passes on. In this case selection is all, or almost all, as space does not allow for extensive description or interpretation. Nor is there much point in attempting to give a general impression of a show, as there is nothing to hold it together, unlike a group show with a programme or a manifesto to consider. The only possible general comment is limited to a comparison of one year with another, or of one exhibition with some comparable one.

The phrase-maker is thus king. An apt combination of noun and adjective, a *bon mot*, an evocative phrase, is as much as an artist can hope for and a reader can expect. The reader's only remedy is to go to the exhibition. In Victorian Britain or France during the Second Empire the critic had some influence over taste. It is doubtful how much influence a critic has today, though high claims are made for Clement Greenberg as the promoter of American Abstract Expressionism. A cynic will remember that research into the opinion-forming powers of newspapers has tended to conclude that readers expect to have their existing views confirmed. If so, the power of critics may be no more than the listings services offered in the papers or on posters, while real power can be found in the organisation of the art market.

A different sort of exhibition which has had some success in attracting attention, and thus newspaper coverage, is the prize competition. Here the critic is absolved from making judgements of his own by the need to report what a jury has decided about prizes. The critic's standing is thereby reduced, and the description or evaluation of the prize works is less than likely to be uninfluenced by their new position.

How then is the reader of art criticism best advised to use criticism to follow the fortunes of artists? One policy is to try to see more than one review of any exhibition. The notice board at a show where notices are pinned up will give the general idea of what sort of reviews have been written. It is a usual feature of such a comparison that there is a basic level of information which is common to most of the reviews, and it is the mark of a skilful critic to have worked in some personal assessment of works, or some individual response to the show as a whole. The data common to all reviews can be discounted as being neither criticism nor evaluation. The nuggets of real criticism are those views which are evidently based on personal reactions and responses.

THEMES AND ARGUMENTS

Articles on exhibitions sometimes glide away into topics which have little to do with the art on display. This will be disappointing for a reader who expects at the least some evaluation of the shows. The arguments put forward can be interesting in themselves, but their drift is often towards making the context of the art shown more understandable. Art politics or cultural history are favourite themes for such reviewers, apart from the spectrum of cognate disciplines which may be the specialities of writers who are only occasionally concerned with art.

Thematic articles are likely to be found in two sorts of periodicals, general magazines and academic journals, either interdisciplinary or of specialist disciplines. Valuable interpretive ideas may be found in journals of psychology, aesthetics, philosophy, history, religion, sociology, anthropology, even medicine and biology, although these may not be matched up with descriptions and evaluations of art. Such articles may not start with art; as Rudolf Arnheim said about his book, *Art and Visual Perception*, he applied principles of visual perception to examples taken from the arts. Only in his more recent work *The Power of the Center*, published in 1988, has he been looking from art to the resources offered by psychology.

One of the intriguing questions about any thematic article is what motivated the writer? Some articles are clearly written as a by-product of teaching, perhaps adapted from lectures or intended to form part of a book. Others are contributions to a current debate, using art as a theme, in discussing political issues, for example. Some thoughtful articles aim to make connections, perhaps across national and language frontiers, or between disciplines. The reader's criteria for judging articles will vary accordingly.

Art politics can prove a rewarding topic for a journalist. Tom Wolfe's book *The Painted Word* is a witty example of the genre; it originally appeared in *Harper's Magazine*, before being made into a book in 1975. There are good satirical illustrations by the author, paralleled by a text which makes fun of American criticism, Abstract Expressionism and Pop Art.

Wolfe puts his argument as follows: 'What I saw before me was the critic-in-chief of the *New York Times* saying: In looking at a painting today, "to lack a persuasive theory is to lack something crucial". I read it again. It didn't say "something helpful" or "enriching" or even "extremely valuable". No, the word was *crucial.* In short: frankly, these days, without a theory to go with it, I can't *see* a painting.'[9]

This overpraise of criticism justifies the book's title, *The Painted Word*; elsewhere, the book has racy descriptions of New York art life, and a headcount by the author of those he considers care about art. A diagram of the art world, according to Wolfe, would be made up, in addition to the artists, of 'about 750 culturati in Rome, 500 in Milan, 1,750 in Paris, 1,250 in London, 2,000 in Berlin, Munich, and Düsseldorf, 3,000 in New York, and perhaps 1,000 scattered about the rest of the world. That is the art world – a mere hamlet – restricted to *les beaux mondes* of eight cities.'[10] What Wolfe provides is art criticism in a sardonic mode, created by parodying others.

One of Wolfe's targets is the critic Greenberg, about whom an apologist has gravely asserted: 'The significance of Clement Greenberg cannot be overestimated. He is the designer and subtle manipulator of modernism, which is the single most important and influential theory of modern art.'[11] Greenberg wrote exhibition reviews for *The Nation* during the 1940s, but his lasting reputation comes from a collection of his articles, including some more thematic pieces for *Partisan Review*, in a book published in 1961 with the title *Art and Culture.* Greenberg's name has a special glamour because of his successful advocacy of Abstract Expressionist artists against 'the dominance of the School of Paris', as Barbara Reise wrote. Moreover, 'His role shifted easily from the alienated critic writing art columns for intellectual magazines to an impresario in the New York art-world judged by his commitment to a specific type of art and respected for its ultimate (commercial and influential) success.'[12]

Greenberg's articles are marked by a confident authority, as in the following passage.

> Looser paint-handling, combined with what remained an essentially Cubist sense of design, drawing, layout, was what artists as different as Gorky and Pollock had in common during the mid-1940s. If the term 'Abstract Expressionist' means anything verifiable, it means painterliness: loose, rapid handling, or the look of it; masses that blot and fuse instead of shapes that stay distinct; large, conspicuous rhythms; broken color; uneven saturations or densities of paint; exhibited brush, knife, finger or rag marks – in short a constellation of physical features like those defined by Wölflinn when he extracted his notion of the *Malerische* from Baroque art. As we can now see, the displacing of the 'linear' and quasi-geometrical as the dominant mode in New York (and Parisian) abstract art after 1943 offers another instance of that cyclical alternation of non-painterly, or linear, and painterly which has marked the evolution of Western art since the sixteenth century.[13]

A more political theme for an article is the issue of subsidies for the arts. The sticking point is, generally, who should get this encouragement? The National Endowment for the Arts in the United States has been under heavy fire for its choices, as is usual for Ministries, whether in nineteenth-century France or the present-day USSR. Choices for subsidies are in themselves art critical judgements, just as commissions are, and public debate can become enflamed over commissions. The art critic has no decisive voice in such controversies, though arguments can be made by analogy from existing art to what may be done.

Another form of article which can include art criticism is a theoretical paper. For example, the cultural theory of the 1970s, according to an article by Victor Burgin on *The End of Art Theory*, drew predominantly on feminism, Marxism, psychoanalysis and semiotics. In his view the independence of modernism in art has been 'further subverted by the demonstration of the necessarily "intertextual" nature of the production of meaning'.[14] Cultural history and theory, it has to be said, have very extensive agenda, and art criticism is perhaps only a sub-paragraph under a secondary heading. The reader may be doomed to disappointment in reading through an article with wide contextual terms of reference if looking for something as simple as descriptions of works of art, their interpretation and evaluation.

Articles of synthesis between art and other subjects may include important art criticism. Literary theory is at present in demand as a point of reference for writing on the visual arts. Articles on this sort of theme may appear in art periodicals, but are just as likely to be found in other journals, on literature, say, or history. What is most likely to be useful in such material is the chance that inferences can be drawn by the reader, seeing a similarity in a problem elsewhere with a question in the visual arts.

7

As things are: description

THE OBJECT OF ATTENTION

The description of an object is not a simple task. An art object is especially difficult for the critic, as there are many ways in which its description can be approached. Let us take a sculpture, depicting a girl's nude figure, of bronze, sixty-three inches high, called *The Dance Step*, by the Italian sculptor Giacomo Manzù. The girl's slim figure, small breasts, and pony tail haircut are those of an adolescent, while her pose, one foot at right angles to the other, is just a little away from the third position in classical Western ballet.

Eduard Trier chose to illustrate this figure in *Form and Space*, in which he limits himself to two observations: it is a product of refined artificiality (in comparison with the elemental force of Marino Marini's sculpture), and the girl (in comparison with a figure by Marcello Mascherini) is 'more reserved, displays a leisurely elegance in her arrested dance step'.[1]

Manzù's girl is thus described by Trier first as an artefact, and then as a person; his terms of reference are the characteristics of two other sculptors. This skimpy description is not unusual in a survey, and the missing positive evaluation he might have made is only implied in his choice of the sculpture for inclusion in his book. No other information is given about the work itself, although there is a brief biographical note about the sculptor. There are a number of other ways in which the work could be described, for example its colour, its surface, or whether it is unique. The pose, expression and figure of the girl could have been more fully interpreted in several ways beyond the comparisons with the work of two of Manzù's Italian colleagues. Who is she? We do not know her name, though it is unlikely that the sculptor did not have a model.

The girl is anonymous, just as are the models for some religious scenes described by Giorgio Vasari. He wrote about the famous frescoes by Giotto in the church of St Francis of Assisi:

> In truth the work exhibits great variety, not only in the gestures and postures of the different figures, but in the composition of each subject, besides which it is very interesting to see the various costumes of those times and certain imitations and observations of Nature. One of the most beautiful of these represents a thirsty man, whose desire for water is represented in the most lively manner as he kneels on the ground to drink from a spring, with such wonderful reality that one might imagine him to be a real person.[2]

Vasari praised Giotto's ability to represent things visible, a highly usual expectation in the tradition of Western art. Paintings which describe the natural world are indeed easiest for the critic to describe, since any observer can compare an object seen with the same thing depicted. This comparison may form the crucial part of a description; later on, using comparison as a criterion, that a portrait should look like the sitter, that landscape should look natural, and the objects in a still life should be identifiable, a critic can use it as part of an evaluation.

A still life is in some ways an ideal picture to describe, as a firm basis can be found in a catalogue of its components. A list can even rise to evoking the mood of a picture, as in this description by the Goncourt brothers of Chardin's subjects; 'He introduces into his pictures his wash-basin, his mastiff puppy, the objects and the creatures to which he is accustomed in his home . . . the pure simple features of the working middle class, happy in its tranquillity, its labour and its obscurity. The genius of the painter is the genius of the home.'[3]

People in pictures can be more problematic to describe, since they may not be identifiable, a special difficulty with portraits. The activities of people in pictures can be equally puzzling. Indeed, if the story enacted in a picture is not known, quite wrong inferences can be drawn from what is perceived. The reader of a description needs therefore to be careful about accepting as a description anything more than is actually visible on the canvas or in the sculpture.

Within a particular culture, a description can naturally go further in identifying a devout picture of a Virgin and Child, or a dancing figure with six arms as Siva. The Christian painting may be at once a holy picture and a convincing representation of a woman tenderly cradling her son, seen in front of a north Italian landscape. The Siva statue has no such direct representational reference.

A critic unfamiliar with a culture will have trouble in formulating a description of a work. Take African sculpture, much admired by European artists in the twentieth century for its bold forms, not representational of the human figure in a Western sense. Frank Willett in *African Art* comments:

> African sculpture has been commonly described as frontal, i.e. the figures are symmetrically disposed about a vertical axis. There are, of course, exceptions to this, but asymmetrical pieces are uncommon. Because of their frontality African figure sculptures are commonly photographed or drawn full face, concealing the fact that the sculptor has paid a great deal of attention to the profile view.[4]

Then he says something about the formal appeal of this sculpture to twentieth-century Western taste, because of its freedom from the canon of realism:

> It is easy enough to analyse the formal characteristics of African sculpture in terms of vertical, horizontal or diagonal emphases; of relative naturalism or abstraction; of rounded, angular or cubic elements; or in terms of tensions, rhythm and movement, and this is certainly an enjoyable and satisfying experience, since African sculptors have achieved a remarkable level of expression in what has been called 'purely sculptural' form.

This account raises two significant issues about description; one is parallel to comments on photography which have already been made. In seeing African sculpture reproduced, the reader can remember that this art is to an extent being misrepresented by photography. Secondly, the formal analysis which is second nature to a Western critic can be fruitful, even though it could be argued that this is a way of interpreting the objects of an unfamiliar culture rather than a description.

A further type of difficulty arises in descriptions of works produced in Far Eastern cultures. While a Western eye is familiar with the process of looking, as it were, through an image to what it represents or means, an Eastern critic looks also at the surface of a painting or a drawing, in which a poem or other calligraphic element may form an integral part of the work. Chinese painting and calligraphy are visual arts on much of an equal footing. A Japanese example is the *surimono*, a friendly greeting for the New Year through a drawing and a message which complement each other. Here a measure of interpretation is integral to the work itself.

The long-standing popularity of Japanese woodcut prints in the West has somewhat disguised differences in approach. The undeniable and striking formal qualities of composition in works by such masters as Hokusai and Hiroshige have had demonstrable effects on late-nineteenth- and twentieth-century European art. Nevertheless, such prints are not justly reduced even in description to mere compositional terms. The materials used, for example, merit attention rarely given to paintings in the West whose science is intended to create an illusion.

What the reader of criticism deserves, in sum, is an appropriate description. There are some aspects of a work of art which can be measured, for example its size, natural or chemical composition, and some facts can be discovered about works through specialist techniques such as infra-red photography. These may or may not have significance; what needs to be certain is that descriptions are accurate, for if they are wrong, deductions from them will be valueless. A fragment from an altarpiece cannot be appraised in just the same way as an independent portrait; and a craftsman's skill is esteemed more accurately when the materials used are rightly identified.

PERCEPTION

How a spectator views an object is also not a simple matter, despite this century's increased knowledge of the psychology of perception. A difficulty is that psychology has narrow terms of reference which can give only a few useful results, for example on the question of illusion. A classic example of exposition, though not uncontroversial, is E. H. Gombrich's *Art of Illusion*. This usefully explores some of the resolvable questions, in particular those of crucial interest to students of landscape and the human figure.

One aspect of illusion is perspective, much valued in the Western tradition. Three sorts of perspective are identified by Leonardo da Vinci in his treatise on painting, as follows:

> The first deals with the reasons of the (apparent) diminution of objects as they recede from the eye, and is known as Perspective of Diminution: the second contains the way colours vary as they recede from the eye: the third and last explains how objects should appear less distinct in proportion as they are more remote. And the names are as follows: Linear perspective, the perspective of colour, the perspective of disappearance.[5]

The Renaissance became enamoured of perspective, indeed Vasari thought that Paolo Uccello took it too seriously. He wrote:

> Paolo Uccello would have been the most delightful and imaginative genius since Giotto that had adorned the art of painting, if he had devoted as much pains to figures and animals as he did to questions of perspective, for, although these are ingenious and good in their way, yet an immoderate devotion to them causes an infinite waste of

time, fatigues nature, clogs the mind with difficulties, and frequently renders it sterile where it had previously been fertile and facile.[6]

But when Uccello died in his eighties, 'He left a daughter who could design, and a wife who used to say that Paolo would remain the night long in his study to work out the lines of his perspective, and that when she called him to come to rest, he replied, "Oh what a sweet thing this perspective is!" '

Mathematical perspective of a Renaissance sort had not been used in European medieval art, where the size of a figure often derives from the person's importance, God the Father never being small. A perspective may be used which reverses the convergence of lines in the distance; instead, lines of perspective converge in front of the viewer, an unexpected phenomenon for a twentieth-century spectator used to photographs.

Again, in Chinese art perspective is different from its treatment in the West. There is one sort of Chinese perspective, seen as in the West from a level viewpoint, but this is only one of three treatments of space representation. It can be identified with *p'ing yuan*, when one is able to see 'from the near parts to the furthest parts'.[7] In this, as in Western perspective, the horizon line is somewhere below the middle of the picture. One alternative Chinese perspective is *shen yuan*, in which the viewer is placed as if on a hill, and the horizon line is thus high up, almost a bird's eye view. The third perspective is *Kao yuan*, in which the viewer is looking up towards a mountain scene, as William Willetts puts it, 'through successively receding heights represented by flat parallel planes, each with its own horizon'.[8] The point of making these comparisons is that artistic practices affect how a critic should describe a landscape. Suppose a scene is said to be in correct perspective? This description could mean several different things. Yet such a comment may need to be made, nevertheless, to point out the quality of a picture. The critic who pays little notice to perspective or other means of representing the natural world will deprive a reader of help in enjoying the exceptional beauty of the natural appearance of Impressionist pictures, whose qualities are inspired by scientific understanding of light and its effects.

In a different sort of context, what appears to be an abstract design, devoid of reference to the natural world, may in fact be a stylisation of a person, an animal or an imagined figure. The totems of American Indians, the carvings of Inouk, ancient bronze ritual vessels from China, and many more examples can be found through the world and the centuries. Most African sculpture is not in this category, as characteristically the masks and ritual objects of Africa are more evidently human or animal in appearance. Care has to be taken by a critic in any of these cases to describe works as definitely as possible. A totem, for example, can be described first as it appears, then as an object which has stylised figures in the sculpture.

A further example of abstract form which is not mere pattern is Tantric art. A Tantric painting or drawing has a spiritual purpose, to assist the user in meditation. As a sound is a mantra, so an image is a yantra, the two used together making a powerful combination for spiritual exercises. A description of a Tantric painting as a linear diagram may seem uninteresting, but then the effect of such a picture is not meant to be pleasure for the eye alone, but for religious use.

WAYS OF DESCRIBING

We have thought so far mainly about verbal descriptions, the stock in trade of the art critic. There are other ways of description, which may incidentally be employed by a critic, or can be useful to a reader as a check on the validity of a verbal description.

In chapter 4, on monographs, there were some comments on the photography of art as a complement to criticism; there are some other issues about how accurate or misleading photographs can be. Perhaps this is the more important in the late twentieth century now that this means of image-making is so familiar that some people actually imagine that a photograph shows the world as it is. In truth, the camera is a ruthless editor of visual information; this can be made plain by looking at a picture, say of the eighteenth century, and comparing it with a contemporary print, perhaps an aquatint, and a modern photograph. The images carry different information. The physical make-up of dots in a photograph differs from the lines and granular surface of the aquatint; the aquatint's variations describe the picture more eloquently. The art of civilisations other than that of the West are now more readily visible through photography, and within the limitations of the medium, usefully so. But what do tourists actually see during a visit to India?

Are they able to look without too dominant a preconception coming from the Western tradition? There are amusing archaeological records in the nineteenth century of the inability of even trained artists to record what they saw; Assyrian figure sculptures, for example, were recorded as having unmistakably classical Greek features by an artist in the employ of the archaeologist Sir Henry Layard.

A different sort of description is an artist's copy of a work. Copying was a well-paid occupation in nineteenth-century France, since private collectors and travellers were happy to have copies of pictures in famous collections like the Louvre. Copying was also part of an artist's training, practised by Delacroix and Géricault, Cézanne and Renoir. At the age of sixty-eight Ingres made copies of masterpieces. Accurate copies might be made, but there is in addition a category of interpretive copy, where the artist copies those elements which most appeal to him. This sort of copy is at the same time description and interpretation, the salient points being brought out by the copyist, who gains greater understanding of a masterpiece by his work.

It is not altogether satisfactory to call a print by an artist on the same theme as one of his paintings a description. After all, it is an original work in itself. Nevertheless, the differences between painting and print may be instructive, and help the interpretation of both. By other forms of reproduction an image may be more or less degraded, so that nothing can be learnt from them.

There remains the courtesy paid by one art to another, as in the poem which Baudelaire suggested might be a high form of critical writing. Or it may be music, as in Mussorgsky's composition which he entitled 'Pictures from an Exhibition'. These forms of art, however, can generally be believed to have only a friendly connection with their inspiration, which, indeed, is normally only the starting point for the exercise of the talent of the musician or the poet. It was a Romantic notion that there were resonances in the natural world and art; and it was Schiller who argued that music, the visual arts and poetry 'always become . . . similar in their action on the mind'.

THE AESTHETIC EXPERIENCE

Describing the object is not the only sort of description that a reader can expect from a critic. The critic may be willing to share an experience with the reader, sometimes only of the circumstances in which a work was seen, as might be included in a personality article; but on other occasions the critic may give a fuller account of a personal response to a work of art. This then becomes not a description of the object itself, but of the critical appreciation or dislike that the work gives rise to. A hairline distinction exists between this description of personal experience and the evaluation of a work. In an evaluation the critic may put personal feeling aside.

What is an aesthetic experience? The question has puzzled generations of Western historians, critics and philosophers for at least two centuries because of the difficulty of disentangling the aesthetic from other responses. A pragmatic view is that an aesthetic experience is what is described as such, and as there are varieties of religious experience, so there may be varieties of aesthetic experience.

Let us join an American educationalist talking to children about their understanding of art. Michael J. Parsons describes his work in *How We Understand Art*. He can introduce us to some American girls and boys who spoke up about what they noticed and liked. If Andy thought a drawing by Paul Klee looked 'sort of funny', he said so. Parsons has some sensible reflections about how the children's comments can be connected with psychological theory.

Parsons outlines five stages of cognition, which he has based on the scientific work of Kohlberg. Other writers have used different theories, for example those of Piaget. Herbert Read in his book *Education through Art* took up the categories of types put forward by Jung. But for our present purpose, Parsons' young friends will be good witnesses for us. At first, Parsons tells us, 'young children rarely find fault with paintings, no matter what their subject or style . . . they allow associations and memories freely to enter their response. The common characteristic is the happy acceptance of whatever comes to mind . . . paintings are a stimulus to pleasant experience.'[9] This personal and inner satisfaction gives way at the next stage to taking account of the viewpoints of others, and the experience of others. Following this, the children come to realise that pictures are part of a tradition; finally, children may be prepared to make a judgement going beyond an individual culture.

This subtle scheme has advantages over simpler divisions. Picasso's *Guernica* is 'OK for some but I don't like it', as a young boy put it. The first stage starts with a simple liking, 'I love blue', 'My favourite colour is yellow'. In the next stages there is pleasure to be found in identifying subjects, and in discovering that pictures can convey messages expressively. The idea that art is part of a tradition is a further step. Whereas in stage two, detail is a pleasure, in stage four the refinement of imagery and simplicity may be enjoyed. Comparisons between cultures become possible in the last stage.

This theory of stages in understanding art is helpful, and it will immediately be realised that the first two stages fit in with description, the next two with interpretation, while the final stage is judgement. The theory is not so useful in defining the quality or strength of responses, and is no help in analysing the interactions of responses. The theory is nevertheless of a sort which can be of real use in a classroom.

Perhaps the most usual description of aesthetic experience in the last hundred years has occurred when the critic has been faced with the need to react to one isolated work of art. It was Roger Fry's contention that an object, say a bunch of carrots on a market stall, could be viewed in a practical way as something to eat for supper, or aesthetically. This distinction can be backed up by philosophy and aesthetics, and descriptions can be found of the resultant moments of vision or epiphanies. Our concern, however, is not with the difficulties of aesthetics, but only with what a critic writes of aesthetic experience, and how useful such an account may be. This is an aspect of description, while it can be suggested that other religious, political or social concerns are more properly matters of interpretation.

Unfortunately it is often the case that writers do not allow themselves to be so free in autobiographical disclosures as to say exactly how they felt on seeing some work of art. While they may describe the work, they avoid describing their own responses to it.

Two honest critics can be given as exceptions, the first a Japanese who recorded a negative reaction to a picture which did not come up to his standards of meaningful symbolism. He is Toru Torada, and the picture, *Blue*, by Kumai Sugai. 'Suddenly I was confronted by a huge and altogether indescribable blue figure wearing a red hat. But the painting said nothing at all to me as I stood gazing at it. It fulfilled none of my expectations and seemed to be merely trying to make me laugh at the fact that it had left me standing there grasping at nothing. And that was all there was to it.'[10]

By contrast, here is a comment by an anthropologist who went to see the work of Mark Rothko. 'At the end of the exhibition, looking at a painting entitled *Black on Grey*, and dated 1970, I tried to pay attention, "bare attention", to its visual forms. But what I knew and felt kept interfering.'[11] What the anthropologist Jacques Maquet knew was that a few weeks after finishing this sombre painting, Rothko committed suicide. Questions and comments, feelings and comparisons kept interrupting his attempt at contemplating the work. Then, 'Instead of struggling in vain to prevent them from reaching my consciousness, I stepped back, as it were, and let thoughts and feelings come and go. I noticed their appearance and also noticed that, left alone, they disappeared too. My previous attempts at getting rid of them had had the effect of reactivating them. I was still overwhelmed by the painting, but I was now aware that I was overwhelmed, and this, somehow, seemed to establish a distance between this emotion and me.'

8

In all respects: interpretation

MYTHS

Part of the task of a critic is to ensure that works of art are understood. This understanding may be a simple appreciation that a work resembles the natural world, say a landscape; in this straightforward case the critic can move on quickly to the qualities of skill and mind that the artist has brought to a descriptive task.

The subjects of other works of art are more complex, and may depend on cultural knowledge. The story of the announcement by the angel Gabriel to Mary that she would become pregnant and bear a child, Jesus, is known to all Christians. The critic writing for a Christian readership has no need to identify this familiar story, and can concentrate on how it is presented. A picture of the Annunciation is an affirmation of religious belief, and will inspire religious reflections in the mind of a believer. The non-believer may also find such a picture beautiful in itself, and an inspiration for reflection.

Similarly, a Hindu believer will have no difficulty in identifying a pastoral scene in which Krishna, traditionally depicted with bluish skin, is enjoying the attentions of the women of Brindaban who fell in love with him; nor is there a problem for a westerner in enjoying such a picture. More problematic is a representation of the origins of the world; here in an Indian example of the eighteenth century, the painter unknown, a man is seen with a woman in intercourse above him; from the pair springs a lotus leaf on which is a beheaded blue figure, head on a dish in his left hand, with attendant nude female figures with swords on either side. A Hindu knows that the loving couple are Vishnu and Mahalaksmi, and the seated figure on the lotus is Mahavidya Chinnamasta, and can use this knowledge in meditation. Without this knowledge, a spectator may find difficulty in passing through the unaccustomed strangeness of the image to recognise its effectiveness and quality.

One definition of a myth is a divine story, and in this sense the myth affirms religious belief. The Christian devotion of early Italian masters of the Renaissance is plain to see in images which eloquently tell stories from the Biblical testaments. Abstractions from figures and forms of the natural world, as seen in twentieth-century art, are more difficult to interpret. For example, Matisse decorated a chapel at Vence. In this building he treated the life of Christ in black line drawing on white tiles in a simple diagrammatic form. Perhaps the nuns worshipping in the chapel needed no more than these brief mementoes of their faith, and certainly the aesthetic effect of the interior in which variations of light filter in through coloured glass makes up a special atmosphere. Matisse's summary reminders are nevertheless in sharp contrast to the explicit nature of Renaissance images. Artists may take the view that a myth will be immediately understood; if they do so, it falls to a critic or a historian to explain the imagery to the uninformed.

Another sort of theme in use during the Italian Renaissance was classical myth, which performed two different functions. On the one hand, these pictures and sculptures of Pagan myths were outside Christian belief but were flattering to Italians who considered their culture comparable with that of classical times; on the other, moral meanings could often be read into the stories. It is the difficult task of an art historian to assess how such works were enjoyed and interpreted, whether the artists' intentions can be known and if they were successfully carried out; sometimes a picture remains enigmatic, a happy hunting ground for interpreters. In other instances even if a final truth cannot be discovered, at least the careful historian can clear away misconceptions.

A further way in which an art historian can help a reader is to demonstrate where there is a shift from one emotional attitude to another. In his book, *Meaning in the Visual Arts*, Erwin Panofsky made a point of distinguishing between iconography and what he termed iconology:

> In the fourteenth and fifteenth centuries, for instance (the earliest examples can be dated around 1300), the traditional type of the Nativity with the Virgin Mary reclining in bed or on a couch was frequently replaced by a new one which shows the Virgin kneeling before the Child in adoration. From a compositional point of view this change means, roughly speaking, the substitution of a triangular scheme for a rectangular one; from an iconographical point of view, it means the introduction of a new theme to be formulated in writing by such authors as Pseudo-Bonaventure and St Bridget. But at the

> same time it reveals a new emotional attitude peculiar to the later phases of the Middle Ages.[1]

A little later he states his intention 'to revive the good old word "iconology" wherever iconography is taken out of its isolation and integrated with whichever other method, historical, psychological or critical, we may attempt to use in solving the riddle of the sphinx'. This passage was published fifty years ago, but it retains importance for the art of criticism.

For a twentieth-century example, Kokoschka painted the classical story of Prometheus bringing fire from the gods to man. The iconography is the story, but the interpretation of the story can be various. Only an unwise critic would pronounce on the artist's meaning, since the picture's owner explained that Kokoschka used to take people to see the picture, and on different occasions explained it in different ways.

Where a modern painting treats a myth, the artist's attitude to the myth is pre-eminent for its interpretation. However, the critic's task can be complicated if the artist's intentions are concealed in the work by deliberate ambiguity, and if the artist keeps silent, or gives misleading answers when asked questions. Perhaps the critic's assumption in looking at a new work is that a picture or a sculpture is likely to have no function to do with belief.

A different sort of problem occurs when the artist attempts to invent a myth. Stories told by novelists and poets are sometimes described as myths, which literary critics occupy themselves in interpreting; but they are less usual in art. An invention can only be interpreted by the author, it may be thought. However, sometimes the artist may be prepared to allow interpretation by all-comers; sometimes an intermediate position is taken by an artist who renounces authorial possession to suggest that a work has a life of its own after its creation, a life over which he or she has no further control. Some Surrealist works have this sort of character, and even where there may have been a discoverable starting point, a liking for mystification may conceal this origin. The viewer is thus left with an unexplained work, to which meanings and interpretations can be affixed.

Judith E. Stein, for example, writes of elusive reality and enigmatic layers of significance in discussing *August, 1985* by Cheryl Laemmle. The catalogue in which this piece of criticism appears has a coloured plate of the work, so there is no need to explain that the picture is dominated by two standing wooden birds:

> Two wooden decoys are set against a dramatic, cloud-streaked sky, bordered by a sepulchral compartment containing a small dead bird. The bright target displayed on the breast of the eyeless, more colourful lure is echoed in the circular carvings on its spherical pedestal. The poignant trophies of dead game and wild birds that

> bedeck its chest like medals are metaphors for the thoughtless destruction of the environment.[2]

Laemmle's mythical birds are evidently believed by the critic to be evil agencies, with specific intents. Sixty years earlier, as Surrealism began, other birds menaced spectators from the pictures of Max Ernst. The interpretation of Marcel Jean is as follows:

> The creatures released by Max Ernst's imagination are new gods. If they have any relation with the past it is on the plane of poetic analogy; they are not more or less transposed imitations of a pre-existent document. Men in ancient times believed that insects and serpents sprang spontaneously from the damp earth; Ernst gives a positive force to this old illusion: in his hands, pictorial material comes alive and gives birth to new reptiles, mantises and hitherto unknown birds of prey.[3]

The word myth is used in a variety of ways, in some of which an element of the divine is absent. So far we have excluded the facts of history or the inventions of fiction, which sometimes are described as myths, or are said more loosely to have mythical status. It is to these we must turn next.

HISTORIES AND FICTIONS

While myths have a special place in the subject matter of art, paintings can also be more matter-of-fact as illustrations, telling the stories of history, or complementing the narratives of poetic or prose fictions. Such pictures have a more direct relationship to their subjects than pictures of myths, as they need not carry the weight of religious devotion or contemplative reflection.

The high-tide mark of Western historical illustration was the nineteenth century, when European nation states were eager to define their proud and independent nationality. School history books were embellished with illustrations of the great; the official academy exhibitions had space reserved for historical reconstructions of famous events; the streets and squares of European cities were adorned with statues of the makers of their countries, famous military or naval leaders, and other celebrated historical figures.

This fashion for historical narrative did not make major demands on the talents of artists, even if a Delacroix could rise splendidly to the opportunity of an important state commission. A concern about historical detail, and the elaborate mechanics of large-scale figure compositions are factors which make for dullness in many of the paintings answering these particular social and political needs.

The relationship of fiction to art can be regarded with more interest. Whereas historical events are recorded in other ways, such as film and photographs, fiction needs interpretation and finds it through book illustrators. The perfect match of artist and writer is sometimes found, so that it is difficult to dissociate say, *Alice's Adventures in Wonderland* from Tenniel; and however excellent other drawings may be, Dickens as Boz is linked with Browne as Phiz. Formalist art criticism in the twentieth century has played down the achievements of illustration, partly from a persistent attempt to isolate aesthetic experience from other feelings. This was the approach, for example, of Roger Fry when he wrote of the artist's preoccupation with form, when 'a man's head is no more and no less important than a pumpkin, or, rather, these things may be so or not according to the rhythm that obsesses the artist and crystallises his vision'.[4] In this aesthetic, illustration was a weak virtue, and 'significant form' was all-powerful.

There is more to consider about narratives. Some stories lend themselves, as it is said, to film; on the other hand, whatever the box-office figures may suggest, few if any critics held the view that the Superman comic strip was adequately transmuted into three feature films. Indeed, comic books are especially interesting today as a form of visual narrative.

Comic books command huge readerships world-wide. The recycling of comic-book images as works of art in the United States was an entertaining episode in the history of art. What did it show? That for all the critical emphasis on form, honestly held by writers and artists who asserted their primary interest in the way in which the cartoon images were created, it was in fact a narrative appeal which attracted them.

Or, better, cartoons combine formal and narrative interests, like traditional Japanese art. As a writer on the Japanese courtly tradition commented, the climate of opinion in the industrialised West has seen

> great formalist revolutions in taste over the past century [which] have purged painting and sculpture of major literary content . . . It is hostile even to discussions of the literary or doctrinal dimensions of older arts, since verbal content distracts from the purely visual, formal element. While there is solid justification for the modern bias against literature in art, traditional Japanese would have been puzzled by it. They were accustomed to pictures having a high degree of abstraction, of extremely sophisticated formal effects, while at the same time having a precise, often intensely emotional, literary content.[5]

One of the largest markets for comic books is Japan, where the American post-war occupation encouraged the development of a medium which could build on that strong tradition of Japanese book illustration. Hokusai, best known in the West for a dramatic image of a wave seen in front of the sacred mountain Fuji, was a prolific book illustrator of nearly forty novels of varying length, containing more than 1,500 illustrations.

During the nineteenth century, these were sequential separate images, seen by the reader in parallel with the text. In a former period, as Kenji Toda points out, narratives were painted on scrolls: 'Scroll paintings . . . are to be viewed while they are being unrolled . . . The space that can be covered at a glance as one inspects a scroll cannot exceed two feet. It is the gradual revelation of what is given in a succession of such spaces that constitutes the life of a scroll painting, and the real effectiveness is lost when the whole length is spread before our eyes.'[6] This relationship of text to image is one example among many of the sort of question that a critic may need to consider. In Japan, a further twist to comic-book images was given by Osamu Tezuka, who borrowed cinematographic techniques such as close-ups for his pages.

Tezuka was an artist and a film-maker. Other artists practise as writers, being fluent in different media. Parallels may be sought and found between the work of the literary critic and the art critic. While the critic of poetry may be specially sensitive to form, the critic of a novel will be concerned with the devices of literary narrative, and the means of presentation of character and incident. Here are problems in common with the art critic. Let us instance *Don Quixote*, a literary theme which has had extensive treatment in paintings and illustrations. While Gustave Dore brilliantly depicted the sequence of the Catalan knight's adventures, an artist such as Daumier saw Don Quixote as a figure symbolising the ideals, alas often vain, of a noble spirit, and treats him and Sancho Panza with a mixture of respect and compassion.

The Japanese history of forty-seven samurai who vowed to avenge their master also has more than one level of interpretation; the simpler is a narrative, with picturesque detail in a silent attack in a snowfall by the samurai on the house of Kira Kozuke-No-Suke, their master's enemy whom they killed. At a different level, the story exemplifies a Confucian text, 'Thou shalt not live under the same heaven nor tread the same earth with the enemy of thy father or thy lord'. It is this dramatic religious and emotional content which is expressed in a major play by Chikamatsu.

The limitations of a picture for conveying a sequence of events in life are made more evident by the difficulty of an artist to convey more than a limited range of facial expressions and poses. The novelist has any number of varied means to describe a character, while the artist is limited to a single view. Nor is it necessarily easy to interpret an individual's character from a face – who has not heard of charming, baby-faced murderers? The interaction of persons depicted has something of the common ambiguity of visual images. In this respect, at least, the formalist aestheticians have a point when they wish to filter out some of the human emotions from art, seeing how difficult it is to interpret human situations in paintings.

RITUALS

Rituals reinforce beliefs. Although the twentieth century in Europe and America has seen a religious decline, and art has to some extent become a secular substitute, elsewhere religion has maintained or increased its importance. A ritual element in art thus may perform one of two main functions, either in the service of religion or as an adjunct to artistic activity.

A simple form of visual ritual is drawing a circle within which to practise magic; a more elaborate form of similar drawing is part of everyday life in India, where a householder paints patterns with flour and water on the ground and round the house. Sand-painting by American Indians, also a practice in current use, has a devotional significance, the patterns created on the sand being left to be destroyed by the elements. Such practices are physical activities which leave only temporary visual traces, sharing this character with performances in arts such as music, theatre, and more especially dance.

Bryan Robertson in his monograph on Jackson Pollock makes a point about the artist's 'need to get as close as possible to his actual working materials, to feel the pigment in his hand and to manipulate paint in a new, free, and very direct activity. To achieve the sensual closeness between hand and material of the sculptor, in fact, rather than the orthodox painter, and the modeller rather than the carver. Half-way between painting and indirect modelling is the way the Navaho Indians make their sand-paintings, with the coloured earths spilling and trickling through their fingers or thrown on to the ground from sticks or bowls.'[7] While Pollock's feeling about using materials is common ground with craftspeople's responses, the ritual element was developed further by others.

Some of the rituals practised as art performances have left no permanent traces in artefacts or in the world, although some have been visually recorded or reported. Richard Long is one exemplary artist whose personal performances have included walks through landscape, which he has recorded in photographs. Robert Smithson also took the land for his canvas, but created earth works, some of which have disappeared, including a spiral jetty in a lake. Christo has intervened not in the country but in the town, and has momentarily wrapped up buildings, even the Pont Neuf in Paris. There is, some might say, an element of magical practice in these activities; the artist is seen as a shaman, who wishes to transform the visual world, suggesting by analogy that its present appearance and state needs such a transformation, through the lack of attention which has been paid to it in the past. While Ruskin was regarded as a prophet in Victorian times, inveighing against the evils of inhuman capitalism and manufacture, Smithson's spiral jetty is a signpost to concern with the appearance and well-being of the natural world. This and other poetic gestures of a visual imagination have helped to generate an increased awareness of our world.

An example of criticism of a performance can be given from the catalogue of Alastair MacLennan's recent work. Slavka Sverakova gives a precise description before interpreting a twenty-four-hour performance/installation in Dublin in April 1981:

> Material: Naked and clothed human form head and neck whitened arms and genitals and legs blackened; dead fish on walls and floor; a plastic bag filled with water; water seeping over floor from faulty plumbing.
>
> MacLennan walked round the room, standing still occasionally. He did not eat or sleep. The work's main intention was to present activity without stopping, a form of nonstop 'culture'. The ensuing 'discomfort' was punishment for hubris, but also a sign of commitment on the part of the artist. The old adage that if it hurts it's worth it received its recycling as a strategy for making art in a society which maims itself endlessly.[8]

A reader of such a critique might unwarily suppose that this performance was unprecedented, and difficult to place in a historical context or to compare. Not so. An extensive record of disillusion with twentieth-century society exists, even if not in quite the same form. The unusual feature of MacLennan's performances is the position they occupy, though they are not alone in this either, between drama and art. The art historian can instinctively think of masques and carnivals in Europe, or ritual dances in Africa. Sverakova from her informed knowledge of the artist and his stated intentions can point to the immediate context of his art in his Dundee and Chicago art training, his interest in Zen, and his professional work as a tutor at the University of Ulster.

SYMBOLS

Few words are more troublesome to define than 'symbol' in the context of the visual arts. A symbol can at one level be something that stands for or suggests something else, or it can be a conventional sign. Further, a symbol can be, and often is, an object which is capable of exciting a response. There is an extended philosophical and aesthetic tinge to other meanings of symbols in art and literature. This present brief section is mainly confined to senses of the word by which a symbol may stand for an idea, and to which there is a response, or in which a religious purpose is served. Wider meanings of the word, of course, range into the spheres of philosophy and aesthetics.

The art critic has to be extremely alert to symbols, both to decipher them correctly, and to understand the many responses which they can excite. Let us use the Statue of Liberty as an example. The copper statute by the sculptor Bartholdi was placed on an island in the Hudson River at the entrance to New York harbour in 1889, a gift from France on the hundredth anniversary of the French Revolution. Its double symbolism is of the idea of liberty and of the United States of America. The Statue of Liberty appears as a symbol in all sorts of contexts, favourable or not (as in an anti-American animated film where one of many transformations is that the torch held in Liberty's hand turns into a gun).

Taking another symbol, a statue of Queen Victoria in Glasgow or Toronto, a critic has a number of choices about its interpretation. A bronze sculpture of a sovereign has a function as a symbol of power and authority, so a question that a critic can ask is whether these attributes are successfully expressed by the sculptor. A different approach is to ask whether the statue's existence is underpinned by political power; if so, a change of political circumstances may result in its removal or even destruction.

A third approach is to consider it as a representation of the person concerned – Queen Victoria was rather flattered by her sculptors. A fourth approach is not strictly about the critic's own response to the sculpture, but it may be interesting and informative to see what can be deduced from the statue's siting and other attributes of the figure, such as attendant figures, pedestal or inscriptions.

Some of a critic's considerations of a royal statue are equally applicable to religious images, also vulnerable to changes of power. The destructive fury of iconoclasts has, after all, deprived Christendom of beautiful and remarkable works of art, including the main part of English Gothic sculpture. There is no more decisive mode of criticism than destruction.

Figures of deities are in a separate category for sculpture, in many cultures being presented alone and in a hierarchical frontal pose, to be worshipped by the believer. The setting of a divine figure has always been considered with care, whether it may be the largest bronze statue in the world, the Buddha at Nara in Japan, or the stone statues of Esie in Nigeria. These latter have a particular interest as being a group surrounding a royal figure, now secured in a museum complex, but for long a point of pilgrimage in the forest. An anthropologist, Eva Meyerowitz, regretted the change of location: 'To the neat, museum-minded person the result is no doubt satisfactory, but from the aesthetic point of view it is a tragedy; for it has once and for all ruined a dramatic effect which will never be forgotten by those who, coming out of a narrow bush path, were suddenly confronted with this awe-inspiring spectacle of an assembly, petrified and grotesque, within the vastness of the tropical forest.'[9] Incidentally, the first move under shelter for these figures was far from safety for them, since it has been estimated that 552 heads were pilfered from the House of Images in which they were placed.

A critic confronted by a deity is delicately placed. While a Greek deity has an idealistic human appearance, an Egyptian, Mexican, Hindu or African deity does not, and indeed may appear as a hybrid between man and beast. An appreciative assessment of form may be made, but the intended sway of the divine image will not be realisable by a non-believer.

An image which has been intended from the start as a means of communicating an idea to the viewer is a symbol of a contrasting sort. Posters are useful examples of such images, overtly designed to promote political causes or to assist the sales of commodities. The response intended from these images is clear, to persuade, or to sell. The poster designer Milton Glaser is on record as preferring a good poster to a poor picture, an understandable preference for one in his profession; but the subordination of artistic intent to a political or commercial purpose may equally make the image of interest but the artefact unacceptable. While hate posters against an enemy in time of war may serve their nationalistic purposes, they can justifiably be considered morally and ethically dismaying.

It is in dealing with symbolic imagery that the critic is most likely to be concerned with judgements on society which can be deduced from visual evidence and symptoms of the character of a society. For a critic with ideological commitments these considerations may be more crucial than qualitative judgements on the work of visual art in itself. These are social and perhaps political judgements. Such a critic's primary purpose is not art criticism, but social criticism. Equally, a highly conformist critic may also not be aiming at art criticism, but at producing for readers an acceptance of the political status quo. In neither case is the critic a free agent.

The reader can therefore be suitably cautious in reading this type of criticism. Its intention is not to help the reader to enjoy or appreciate the art which is under discussion, but to promote a point of view in social or political theory. This may be as unhelpful as art-historical writing limited to documentation. Even if the possibilities of interpreting the work of art may be in this way extended, it is the basis for interpretation, not interpretation itself.

9

Judicial enquiry: evaluation

A SIMPLE TEST

Let us go with a young print-maker from a provincial English college to visit Madrid. He has the task ahead of writing on a subject of his choice, and he has decided to study Goya. He has seen examples of Goya's prints, and a few paintings in London, which have encouraged him to go to look at the major paintings in the Prado, and the black paintings in Goya's house.

His preparations for the trip included reading about the artist, whose attitude to the horrors of war our student found sympathetic, and whose artistic courage in portraits and in painting the *Nude Maja* he admired. The sadness of Goya's late years, deaf and living as a hermit, also touched our student. Among the sources he consulted to find out what he might expect in confronting Goya's work in Madrid, he turned to the relevant Pelican history. In the chapter on Goya, Fritz Novotny gave him a succinct account of Goya's career, and several key evaluations of his art. The chapter starts:

> It is doubtful whether the vague superlative 'genius' can be applied to any painter of the real Classicist school. But it is certain that Goya, who was their contemporary, deserves it. Many painters of the period had flashes of genius – for example David, Blake, Fuseli, and Runge – but none of them can be called a genius as unreservedly as Goya can . . . if we deal first with the question of subjects, the moralizing element in Classicist art is also evident in Goya. It is obvious that he shared the basic humanistic ideas and valuations of the period of enlightenment. But he perceived the demonic forces

> underlying them with unusual clarity and reproduced them in his pictures without disguise and without embellishment. Other great minds of his day also knew these things and gave expression to them, for instance, Goethe, Mozart, Beethoven, and Schubert – but, except for Goya, the painters and sculptors perceived them hardly at all.[1]

Thus far, Novotny's assessment is that Goya was 'not alien to his time but expresses its prevailing tendencies'.

There is also the question of placing Goya. Novotny declares: 'Goya was the last great painter in whose art thought and observation were balanced and combined to form a flawless unity. That makes him superior to the Classicists and links him with the great masters of the Baroque.' The six pages of his chapter argue out the details of this judgement.

Our friend has a liking for cartoons. He numbers Daumier among the artists he enjoys, partly for the wit shown in satirising the middle classes, but also for his fluent drawing. So he was pleased to find a few short sentences by a painter making a comparison between the two artists. Charles Ricketts wrote:

> Goya, dramatic, reactionary, and even visionary as he is, found his material at hand; he is aggressively actual and seems to intend to give you nothing but facts. His position is singular – more allied to that of the still little known but extraordinary artist Daumier, the painter of sketches, and improvisations upon the lithographic stone, than to that of any other artist of the Romantic movement in which we find, as it has wittily been put, 'the regret of the world for the Revolution'. In Goya there is no regret, he is the Revolution itself.[2]

His tutor advised him to read the book on Goya by André Malraux, where he found sympathetic understanding of Goya's artistic preferences. He was impressed by Malraux's argument that though Goya did not directly derive material from English caricaturists, it was 'the existence of caricature itself, the existence of a world which, by its nature, escapes "the laws or art" that mattered to him'; and he smiled at Malraux's last sentence, 'And then, modern painting began.'[3] Finally, in consulting books on Goya's prints, he found much praise mingled with interesting detail about the artist's methods.

This reading did not altogether prepare him for the impact that Goya's paintings made on him. The painting of the Eighth of May was not a picture that he could enjoy, nor did it seem to him as a symbol of present life, as one writer had argued. It was an image of violence and pathos. On the other hand, the royal portrait group of the family of Charles IV did not seem to him to justify one art historian's interpretation that Goya had painted a denunciation of the king and his family; he remembered Malraux's view that Goya's colour transmuted his oil pictures in a subtle way.

Once in Madrid, there were other things to see, and at the front of these was the new modern gallery named after the present Queen Sofia. Here a nineteenth-century building housed a collection of twentieth-century art, in spacious surroundings which contrasted painfully with his experience of gallery spaces available in England. For some of the work produced in the last twenty years our student had knowledge of his own to call on. Much was unfamiliar. He used a simple test. After looking at the works in a room, he reconsidered what he had seen, and asked himself what he would wish to take away. The rules of this game that he played were straightforward; there was no restriction of size, nor was there any need to imagine that the work had to fit in with the furnishings of his own living accommodation; and he was allowed, like one of the children outside Salt Lake City, to choose either what he liked (say, because the picture was predominantly yellow), or what he esteemed (even though he was repelled by the subject).

Our student enjoyed his trip. He returned to make a series of pastel dawings inspired by his experience, not unaffected by Goya. From the cornucopia of Madrid's art, however, the work he would have taken away was an installation of boxes by Don Judd; not a work at all related to his own concerns, but of a quality, an unexpectedness and simple elegance to be worth living with.

WONDERFUL THINGS

On 22 November 1922, Howard Carter prised out some stones at the top of the tomb of the Egyptian Pharaoh, Tutankhamun. He was asked, 'Can you see anything?' He replied, 'Yes, wonderful things.'[4] He knew he was looking at the most extraordinary sight seen in the history of archaeological excavation; as his eyes grew accustomed to the light of the candle he was holding, 'details of the room emerged slowly from the mist, strange animals, statues and gold – everywhere the glint of gold'.

It has been the luck of the twentieth century to disinter many works of art, as well as to fish some out of the sea. These discoveries have changed our perceptions of world art, which begins to be a more understandable reflection of human achievements; they are richer than we knew.

In the past, there has been a tendency for the West to centre attention on the main Classical and European art traditions. A corollary has been for critics to have narrow tastes. Even Leo Frobenius, a great scholar of Africa, deceived himself in thinking that west African sculpture found in Ife must have had an origin in Greece. In fact African sculpture can now be shown to have a proud and independent tradition. The Nigerian finds of the Nok culture, for example, which date from between 500 BC and AD 200, include expressive and dramatic terracotta heads which are world masterpieces. As a historian of African art, Werner Gillon, writes:

> Their function could have been connected with funeral ceremonies, ancestor cults or other religious rituals. They might have been conceived as representations of chiefs – though not as their portraits – or as mythical beings and spirits . . . the modelling was always very expert, the figures being built up from elements; with head, torso, coiffure, jewellery and other parts being fashioned separately they were then joined by scoring or key-grooving, and some decorations were added by incisions or by combed, stamped or rouletted impressions. No moulds were used at any time. The resultant sculptures are very sophisticated and most powerful in facial and bodily expressions.[5]

From Africa, the bronzes from Benin have been better known since the seizure of several thousand items in 1897 by a British naval punitive expedition; many of these works remained in Britain, but some were dispersed in Europe. We are speaking here of sculpture of great power and beauty, but of a later date, from the fifteenth century AD. It was sculpture of such quality which led European artists to take more notice of African art, and helped to lead to a critical theory like that of Clive Bell, who was prepared to assert against culture and tradition: 'To appreciate a work of art we need bring with us nothing but a sense of form and colour and a knowledge of three-dimensional space.'[6] Extreme though this view may be, it points to universal opportunities for the critic, not shared by the historian who is more limited by attempting to establish exact facts and convincing interpretations, normally in a limited period of time.

Bell wrote of Primitive Art, a term now tarnished by misuse, and which, it may be hoped, is obsolescent. The term was partly in favour because of an alliance between twentieth-century advanced art and cultures seen as opposed to Western traditions. Byzantine art has been such a culture. Listen, for example, to a writer in 1935 on icons.

> Icon painting thus tended to embody the opposite aim to that which was before the painters of Renaissance Italy, and their technique was equally distinct. The icon painter thus laid in high-lights where the Western painter would shade; there were no attempts at chiaroscuro; colours were used as an intrinsic part of the composition. Western art, again, makes use of everyday figures to express a religious content, whereas the figures of the icon are not of every day; they are themselves fundamentally religious, of the other world rather than of this, the aim being to exalt the spirit to a higher

> plane. They make no appeal to sentiment, being concerned with the life of the mind rather than the life of the body. The aesthetic basis of the art is thus distinct, and it cannot be appreciated unless the normal canons of the Western world are cast aside.[7]

For the art critic, wonderful things do not come only from the West, nor for that matter, only from the East for a Japanese or Indian critic. Through accurate observation and sensitive interpretation a critic may become a good judge of a category of art outside a known tradition, and indeed some affinities may be suggested between traditional practices far apart in time and place. Furthermore, outstanding works have a significance which goes far beyond their original contexts. William Willetts wrote about a landscape painted by the Chinese master, Mi Fei, in AD 1102:

> the whole amounts to a perfect example of atmospheric perspective . . . Economy of means is indeed the most striking thing about this subtle little essay, which has many of the qualities of the sort of painting that came to be called *hsieh i*, or 'writing down an idea'. We would probably call the technique impressionist; yet despite its fugitive atmosphere there is about it an archaic monumentality, related directly to the traditional landscape art bequeathed by the early masters of Northern Sung.[8]

Comparisons between traditions can be overdone, for the reader will inevitably tire of a critic who constantly shows off knowledge of disparate examples, especially if it is not evident what the comparisons are intended to demonstrate. Kenneth Clark is rarely guilty of such overkill, but some readers must have raised an eyebrow over his discussion of Grünewald, Altdorfer and Bosch:

> They are what we now call 'expressionist' artists, a term which is not as worthless as it sounds, because, in fact, the symbols of expressionism are remarkably consistent, and we find in the work of these early sixteenth-century landscape painters not only the same spirit but the same shapes and iconographical motives which recur in the work of such recent expressionists as Van Gogh, Max Ernst, Graham Sutherland and Walt Disney.[9]

CHOICES

The artist as critic has no moral duty to be open-minded, but is able to view the work of others as a resource to use or discard. Writings on art by artists which are most often quoted are those which describe artistic aims and intentions, or general remarks about art; but artists' judgements of other artists are often interesting and apt. We have seen how Reynolds sought to distinguish between the rival merits of Raphael and Michelangelo. In other periods quite decidedly opposing views were held about artists, who gained parties of adherents. In the seventeenth century French artistic opinion was divided between the followers of Rubens and the Poussinists. In the nineteenth century there was a famous conflict between Ingres and Delacroix; a cartoon of the time shows the two painters riding towards one another, paint brushes as lances, their shields with slogans: for Ingres, 'Colour is a Utopia! Long live line!', while Delacroix's shield proclaims, 'Line is a colour!'

The artist is a partisan critic. A classicist artist around 1800 was inevitably affected by the taste for antiquity promoted by Winckelmann. Praise of the Elgin marbles came naturally to his pen. A devotee of the Middle Ages in the middle of the century, imbued with Ruskin, or an ecclesiastical follower of Pugin might be dismissive of the classical tradition, at least in architecture. In reading criticism by an artist, then, the artist's own work is worth remembering. There is no hope of finding an enthusiastic appraisal of Poussin from a Rubenist. Delacroix is an eloquent witness:

> All the young men of this school of Ingres have something of the pedant about them; they seem to think that merely to be enrolled among the party of serious painters is a merit in itself. Serious painting is their party cry. I told Demay that a crowd of people of talent had done nothing worth speaking of because of all those factious dogmas that they get enslaved to, or that the prejudice of the moment imposes on them. So, for example, with this famous cry of *Beauty*, which is, according to the world's opinion, the goal of the arts: if it is the one and only goal, what becomes of men who, like Rubens, Rembrandt, and northern natures in general, prefer other qualities? Demand of Puget purity, beauty in fact, and it is good-bye to his verve. Speaking generally, men of the North are less attracted to beauty: the Italian prefers decoration; this applies to music too.[10]

Or consider Delacroix's reflections on English painting, as he put them down in a letter explaining that he would not care to visit London again.

> Perhaps the impressions I received at that former time might be a little modified today. Perhaps I should find in Lawrence an exaggeration of methods and effects too closely reminiscent of the school of Reynolds; but his amazing delicacy of drawing, and the air of life he gives to his women, who seem almost to be talking with one, give him, considered as a portrait painter, a certain superiority over

> Van Dyck, whose admirable figures are immobile in their pose. Lustrous eyes and parted lips are admirably rendered by Lawrence. He welcomed me with much kindness; he was a man of most charming manners, except when you criticised his pictures . . .[11]

A pleasing feature of some artists' comments is humour, though not often as scathing as George Caleb Bingham's remarks on Landseer:

> A Landseer is captivated by the faithfulness, habits and hairy texture of dogs, and makes them his speciality in Art, being kennelled in his mind, as it were, they exclude other subjects of Art and become the ideal which governs his pencil. When Sidney Smith was requested by a friend to sit to Landseer for his portrait he replied 'Is thy servant a dog that he should do this thing?' His reply was significant of the apprehension justly entertained that the artist could not avoid giving to his portrait something of the expression which more properly belonged to his favorites of the canine species.[12]

Another line of artist's comment is a frank acknowledgement of an artistic debt. This is the character of Henry Moore's words on Brancusi:

> Since the Gothic, European sculpture had become overgrown with moss, weeds – all sorts of surface excrescences which completely concealed shape. It has been Brancusi's special mission to get rid of this overgrowth, and to make us once more shape-conscious. To do this he has had to concentrate on very simple direct shapes, to keep his sculpture, as it were, one-cylindered, to refine and polish a single shape to a degree almost too precious. Brancusi's work, apart from its individual value, has been of historical importance in the development of contemporary sculpture.[13]

Cézanne is well known for being taciturn, and he wrote curt letters. But, according to his biographer Gasquet, the artist could be more expansive, as he records in describing Cézanne looking at Paolo Veronese's *Wedding at Cana* in the Louvre. He spoke of the golden air wrapping the figures in the picture. Then:

> Heavens! the perfect elegance, the exquisite elegance, the daringness of all those flowered stuffs, the stuffs that relate to each other, the arabesques which interlace the flowing gestures . . . Look, let your eyes follow the complete curve of that table. Isn't that beautiful? Isn't it alive? And at the same time isn't it transfigured, miraculous, alive, in another, and yet real world? The miracle is there, the water turned to wine, the world changed to painting . . . One does not

love [these pictures by Veronese] if one looks for literature in them, if one gets excited over the anecdote, the subject . . . I detest all that, these histories, that psychology, these excrescences. Heavens! all that is in the picture, painters aren't imbeciles, but one must see it with the eyes – with the eyes, don't you understand! The painter desires nothing else. His psychology is the relationship of his tones. That is where his emotion lies. That is his personal history, his truth, his profoundness.[14]

BLUNDERS

The most intensely malicious pleasure a reader can get from art criticism is when the critic makes a really bad mistake. The most prominent sorts of blunder are mistaken evaluations, notably of art which later becomes highly prized. Such errors are interesting in themselves, and as examples in the history of taste. The condemnation of the Impressionists by their contemporaries is a spectacular and well-known example. As with movements like Cubism, the trouble mainly lay in faulty interpretation. The critics wrongly believed that a particular set of criteria, appropriate for academic art, could be applied to art with quite different intentions.

The welcome given to the first Impressionist exhibition is famous, including a version of the phrase, 'a child of six could do better'. Here is the quotation from *Le Figaro* on 3 April 1876, by Albert Wolff:

> The Rue Peletier is unfortunate. Following the burning of the opera-house, a new disaster has fallen on the quarter. There has just been opened at M. Durand Ruels' an exhibition which is said to be painting. The innocent passer-by enters and a cruel spectacle meets his terrified gaze. Here five or six lunatics, of whom one is a woman, have chosen to exhibit their works. There are people who burst into laughter in front of these objects. Personally I am saddened by them. These so-called artists style themselves Intransigents, Impressionists. They take paint, brush and canvas. They throw a few colours at the canvas at random and then they sign the lot. In the same way the inmates of a mad-house pick up the stones on the road and think they are diamonds.[15]

Ambroise Vollard quoted some of the disparaging things written about Cézanne with relish; for example, Marcel Fouquier wrote in 1904: 'At first glance, the things that distinguish Monsieur Cézanne's pictures are the awkwardness of their design and the heaviness of their colour. His much vaunted still-lifes are brutal in handling and dull in effect. It has been predicted that they will go one day to the Louvre to keep company with Chardin. Happily that day is still far distant.'[16] Since Vollard was

Cézanne's dealer, he also quoted another hostile critic: 'Some go as far as to pretend that he was a man of genius; business reasons alone might justify such an exaggeration.'[17]

These examples show the critics finding ways to distance the artists from respectable society. The next quotation has religious undercurrents, the offence being to Christian sensibilities. The writer is Charles Dickens, and his subject is the painting by Millais of Christ in the house of his parents:

> You behold the interior of a carpenter's shop. In the foreground . . . is a hideous, wry-necked, blubbering, red-headed boy, in a bed gown, who appears to have received a poke in the hand from the stick of another boy with whom he has been playing in an adjacent gutter, and to be holding it up for the contemplation of a kneeling woman so horrible in her ugliness, that (supposing it were possible for any human creature to exist for a moment with that dislocated throat) she would stand out from the rest of the company as a Monster, in the vilest cabaret in France, or the lowest gin-shop in England . . . This, in the nineteenth century, and in the eighty-second year of the annual exhibition of the National Academy of Art, is what Pre-Raphaelite Art can do to render reverence and homage to the faith in which we live and die![18]

It is tempting, but not altogether relevant, to use monetary values as a way of contradicting these unfavourable assessments of pictures. As it happens, Impressionist painting has seen a steady rise in price, but the Pre-Raphaelites, after a period in fashion, dipped in popularity until their more recent ascent into high prices and esteem. No, the economics of taste are not a lasting way of judging art; there are many imponderables. We are on firmer ground with Delacroix:

> 'In painting, and above all in portraiture,' says Madame Cave in her charming essay, 'it is soul which speaks to soul and not knowledge which speaks to knowledge.'
>
> This observation, more profound perhaps than she herself was aware, is an arraignment of pedantry in execution. A hundred times I have said to myself, 'Painting, speaking materially, is nothing but a bridge between the soul of the artist and that of the spectator.'[19]

If this is so, it is the more disconcerting if a critic finds that the soul speaking turns out to be not an artist, but a forger. The likely fault is not in this case a failure of interpretation, since the forger is likely to be as learned as a critic or a historian, and will have devised an object about whose interpretation there can be little trouble; the failure is more likely to be a failure of observation, that quality which, as we saw, made the reputations and fortunes of a connoisseur like Berenson.

Clearly, if a sculpture proves to have been made in a way which was not possible at the supposed date and place of production, forgery has been established. The dividing line between copies and original works, however, is not so sharply drawn in Eastern art as in the West, say in the case of scroll painting, where it is very difficult to establish absolute authenticity. Pottery and metalwork leave more clues for detective work, something which is also true for African or Pre-Columbian arts.

SUCCESS STORIES

A more benevolent reader may prefer to forget the failures of critics, and rejoice at their successes. These are many. Criticism has been the indispensable means of bringing many artists to public attention, while informed and sensitive art criticism has assisted the building of artistic reputations and financial success. In the 1990s it may seem that such benefits are linked to a booming art market; a more historical approach suggests that though art markets rise and fall, critics have played and can play a valuable intermediary role for artists and their public.

One activity universally attributed to the critic is talent spotting, noting the artists whose promise will be fulfilled in time to come, and suggesting how their talents may develop. Indeed, a Belgian handbook on art and archaeology confined the role of an art critic to this: 'The art critic tries to discover, among the artists of his time, those who show real value; his task consists of classifying, of selecting from the immense production of contemporary art, his mission is to identify the artistic trends of his time.'[20] Though not in agreement with the approach of this book, at least it is a view which is more polite than that of an English art historian, who described art criticism today as a genre which is a 'rigid toadying exercise'.

In fairness to Anita Brookner, the author just quoted, her remark was in the context of a book on French art criticism in the nineteenth century, when, as she rightly commented, art criticism was:

> A career open to all the talents, the field in which the man of letters could not only reveal the extent of his own dilettantism but could say something untoward, let slip some information about himself, his knowledge of, and feeling for, the artist, some cardinal fact about the long slow climb towards interpretation which is the true subject of all criticism.[21]

In *The Genius of the Future* the writers discussed are Diderot, Stendhal, Zola, the Goncourt brothers and Huysmans. For them:

> Painting was either a vehicle for reminiscence or a symbol of an absent friend but it was rarely as important as the train of thought it originally or habitually gave rise to – Stendhal, for example, when talking about individual pictures, can rarely be bothered to stick to the point for more than two sentences.

These critics, according to this view, did not hesitate to describe their own experience as well as the works before them. Another role is the reassessment of an artist who has been unfairly treated or even forgotten. This may partly be a matter of taste, and the cyclical character that its history has followed in past centuries. But it can also be a visionary glimpse of a quality misunderstood at a particular time. Consider, for example, the discovery of Vermeer, partly through the astute judgement of Fromentin; or again, the revaluing of El Greco by Julius Meier-Graefe. Neither of these discoveries fitted with the prevailing canons of taste at the time, but both artists are now firmly established in the pantheon of great Western artists.

10

More than half an eye: critical reading

TECHNIQUE

The previous chapters have been about choices between writings on art. This last chapter is also about discrimination, though its emphasis falls differently. Some of the general considerations that need to be remembered by a reader are outlined, and it is suggested that there is a benefit for a reader to turn writer.

The rules for good reading are well enough known, but the advice of a great English essayist bears repetition. Francis Bacon used to walk with an attendant whose task it was to write down his master's reflections. Perhaps this informal method of composition encouraged pithy expressions, or perhaps his insistence on his words finding a satisfactory Latin form helped his style. Whatever the reason, he talked well about reading:

> Read not to contradict, and confute; nor to believe and take for granted; nor to find talk and discourse; but to weigh and consider. Some books are to be tasted, others to be swallowed, and some few to be chewed and digested: that is, some books are to be read only in parts; others to be read but not curiously; and some few to be read wholly, and with diligence and attention.[1]

These instructions are apt for the reader of criticism, especially the remarks on selective reading. More than a hundred books find a place in this book's bibliography, but not one of them is limited in scope to helping the reader to enjoy or appreciate works of art. On the other hand, some of them contain one or other of the components of criticism in a form which is exceptionally well expressed; catalogues typically print good description, while books connected with other disciplines are strong on interpretation.

A reader following Bacon's rules will be prepared to skim books to find what is useful, not forgetting Bacon's insistence that wisdom does not reside only in books, but can be found 'without them and above them' by observation. So it is with art criticism; through observation a spectator of a work of art can do without art criticism, or can go beyond it; or a reader can make use of art criticism to prepare for an encounter with art; or the astute observer can use criticism to check out personal experiences.

It would be possible to plan a course in art criticism, drawing on Western writing about art, or even writing throughout the world. Headings for such a course are not difficult to sketch out. One alternative would be to consider the history of art criticism, its writing and writers throughout different periods; there are various possible approaches to such a project, though the history of taste would clearly need to play an important role. A second alternative would be to study the theory of art criticism, where philosophy and aesthetics would certainly be significant elements; in this case the critical process, irrespective of period, would be under the spotlight.

PERIODS AND THEORIES

There is one certainty about a reader's search for art criticism: on the way to finding it, a considerable amount of extra reading will take place. This is not only because some art criticism is embedded in other studies, notably art history, but also because reading what art critics have written can be enriched by other knowledge.

Understanding of a historical period is seriously worth attempting. Some critics, perhaps especially blunderers, are confined by their times. Other critics have outstanding powers which can be recognised irrespective of period. One historical limitation is the way in which artistic and critical terms are used. 'Chiaroscuro' is such a term, in use from the seventeenth century, still current when Reynolds delivered his lectures at the Royal Academy, used with a slightly different intonation by Fromentin, and reaching a dead end when it was used as the title for a sketchy autobiography written by Augustus John. Or, consider the term 'picturesque' which was once explained as 'expressive of that peculiar kind of beauty which is agreeable in a picture'; many books and articles have been written about its meaning since its appearance in the work of William Gilpin. Who would now know that a cow was considered more picturesque than a horse?

'The horse in itself, is certainly a nobler animal, than the cow. His form is more elegant; and his spirit gives fire and grace to his actions. But in a *picturesque light* the cow has undoubtedly the advantage; . . . the bones of the cow are high, and vary the line, here and there, by a squareness, which is very picturesque. There is a greater proportion of concavity in them; the lines of the horse being chiefly convex . . . The cow is better adapted also to receive the beauties of light.'[2]

In writing within the last hundred years or so, a reader has to expect that names for styles, such as Baroque, terms like Romantic, or labels for groups and movements will be incorporated as a matter of course. Such words require careful watching for shifts in meaning; one hazard is that new interpretations can readily be built up on words like Baroque, which is itself an attempt to describe common characteristics in works of art; according to a writer's choice, the Baroque may be considered to be an essentially Roman phenomenon, or it may be considered as being European, a geograpical designation which may or may not include England. Critics with a particular interest in the contexts of art may use different terms again, drawn from historical or theoretical writing. The translation of terms from one language to another is a further point of difficulty which can seldom be resolved by looking at a dictionary. Some terms have to be invented in a different language, losing in the process the linguistic context of the original word. This was elegantly remarked by Panofsky, who described art history in Germany as having developed into a technical language; this gave problems for scholars like him who migrated to the United States:

> Every German-educated art historian endeavouring to make himself understood in English had to make up his own dictionary. In doing so he realised that his native terminology was either unnecessarily recondite or downright imprecise; the Germany language unfortunately permits a fairly trivial thought to declaim from behind a woollen curtain of apparent profundity and conversely, a multitude of meanings to lurk behind one term. The word *taktisch*, for example, normally denoting 'tactical' as opposed to 'strategic', is used in art-historical German as an equivalent of 'tactile' or even 'textural'. And the ubiquitous adjective *malerisch* must be rendered, according to context, in seven or eight different ways: 'picturesque' as in 'picturesque disorder'; 'pictorial' (or, rather horribly, 'painterly') as opposed to 'plastic'; 'dissolved', 'sfumato', or 'non-linear' as opposed to 'linear' or 'clearly defined'; 'loose' as opposed to 'tight'; 'impasto' as opposed to 'smooth'.[3]

Critics are also affected by currents of thought in their time, political, social, economic, scientific, literary or philosophical. Readers can often benefit from acquaintance with this background, even though not studying it with the thoroughness which can be expected of an art historical student. This acquaintance may be built up either by reading original sources, or skilled interpretations like *Critical Historians of Art* by Michael Podro, where underlying ideas in history and criticism are exposed. There is no need to multiply instances, for it can easily be realised that idealist philosophy, Marxism, Jungian thought, social anthropology, semiotics or various other viewpoints can also be described.

THE READER TURNED WRITER

What is in fact worth reading? This is a difficult question to answer, not least because every reader has individual standards. Could the reader have written the book? Was nothing learned from it? If so, it was not worth the reading time.

There is no one who cannot write from observation; and as Bacon insisted, wisdom comes from observation, not only from books. The alert reader may like to have a shot at writing a description, and then comparing the result with something published about the same work. Among the differences which may appear is that the reader's account may be fuller and more explicit, since a professional critic is almost sure to have used some shorthand description through labelling or mentioning other artists.

Readers can also brief themselves on interpretations of works of art. A skilful reader may make as good a synthesis of existing views and interpretations as a critic, though the work entailed in finding the necessary sources may be intimidating, and the reader, having no professional compulsion to make a search, may decline the challenge. Further, as the sources for interpretation are secondary material, not the primary experience of an encounter with the work of art itself, good judgement in assessing the value of these sources may be hard to achieve. Here the amateur is at a disadvantage when compared with a professional, who has had more experience of this sort of evaluation. The reader who becomes more deeply interested in interpretations of art, and the social or historical context of art, has a remedy to hand: attendance at lectures or a course which will satisfy those concerns.

The reader turned writer is in a different position when it comes to evaluating works of art. On the one hand, some humility is in order; a great picture judges the critic, not the other way around. A reader may have limitations, whether of experience, of understanding or of sympathy which it is best to admit. On the other hand, no reader has to feel so much over-awed by a work of art that a judgement is impossible. The children outside Salt Lake City were not inhibited in expressing their opinions about art, and what they said can be understood and accepted.

Even if their views show up some inexperience, what they say has a welcome sincerity and vivacity.

Useful advice is available from a number of sources, but perhaps best from Jakob Rosenberg, whose book *On Quality in Art* has some striking things to say to critics. The aim of his book, which was originally a lecture series, is to define those lessons that can be learned by present-day writers from critics in the past. For example, 'It was Vasari who made us realize that our judgement should not be too rigidly restricted by the dominant art theory of our period or by dogmatic historical concepts, but that we should give some leeway to our instinct or intuitive reaction.'[4] Vasari's favourable comments on Titian's late work are instanced. Rosenberg's selection of critics to discuss includes Roger de Piles, Reynolds, Thoré-Burger and Roger Fry. Of the last, Rosenberg writes: 'Finally, it was Roger Fry who gave us an instructive example of how to penetrate into a deeper understanding of works of art through an incisive and perceptive analysis of the formal organization and the technical means employed. In this way he was able to reveal to us the full stature of Cézanne and to extend our understanding of modern art.'

Three firm warnings are given to critics: to avoid quality judgements on whole periods, to avoid judgements on narrow principles or vague criteria, and to be wary of overpraising contemporaries who are fashionable. An important suggestion he makes is that a critic who intends to be discriminating is best advised to compare works of art within a single period, and of a similar style and technique.

Art criticism written by a reader should be unpretentious, for especially if it is written as an exercise, what need is there of pretence? Nor is there any call for elaboration; the course of painting prepared by Roger de Piles can serve as an amusing cautionary tale, with its assessments of artists according to four different criteria: composition, drawing, colour and expression. According to his system of marking Raphael and Rubens scored high with 65 points, while Caravaggio managed only 28, and Giovanni Bellini a mere 24; the two latter artists, incidentally, both scored zero for expression.

To set up a last touchstone of quality for art criticism, the writing of Eugène Fromentin can be used. Fromentin wrote with deep sympathy and attention about Dutch and Flemish painting, interjecting his own understanding of painting techniques and composition in his commentary. He took issue with the idea that Rembrandt was a great colourist, and in writing about the *Night Watch* gave poor marks to Rembrandt's handling of materials and details of the figure of Lieutenant Ruytenburg: 'Notice well how, in their carelessness, affected or not, the form is emphasised, how the foreshortenings are expressed. The touch is heavy and laboured, almost clumsy and hesitating.'[5] This careful scrutiny of the picture may even provoke the reader into disagreement, but Fromentin's praise is not stinted in the 'incontestable interest of the picture', the artist's chiaroscuro:

> The mysterious form par excellence, the most disguised, the most elliptical, the richest in suggestion and surprise, that there is in the picturesque language of painters. In virtue of this it is, more than any other, the form of intimate feelings or ideas. It is light, vaporous, veiled, discreet; it lends its charm to elusive things, incites to curiosity, adds an attraction to moral beauty, gives a grace to the speculation of the inner consciousness. It has a share in fact, feelings, emotions, in the uncertain, the indefinite and the infinite, in dreams and ideals. And that is why it is, as it had to be, the poetic and natural atmosphere in which the genius of Rembrandt never ceased to live.

Fromentin's book was published in 1876, and from a historical point of view is incomplete. Scholarship about the Netherlands in the seventeenth century has moved on since he wrote, so that any schoolboy could find out more about Rembrandt's life than Fromentin knew. Nevertheless, Fromentin's artistic judgement was of a high order, however much his factual information and even technical knowledge may require supplementing from more recent sources. In introducing an edition of the book in 1948, a distinguished Dutch art historian, H. Gerson, commented on changes of taste, but stated his view that 'no artist surely has pronounced a truer and finer judgement on Jacob Ruisdael' than Fromentin, when he described that 'earnest, manly landscape painter, as the artist who "bears the most noble resemblance to his country of all the Dutch painters" '.[6]

Ultimately, the skill of an art critic cannot do more than help the reader. Art criticism is no substitute for personal encounters with the art which criticism can describe, interpret and evaluate. The critic's response to a work will often be imperfectly written, and interpretations may fall short of being persuasive. It may be the critic's hope to have cleared away obstacles to understanding, and the reader's good fortune to have learnt something valuable or interesting.

A final mystery remains in art itself. Everything will never be revealed, felt and understood. 'In art,' warned Braque, 'there is only one thing of value, that which cannot be explained.'[7]

FINDING ART CRITICISM TO READ

Journalism and lectures both reappear in books, making them the types of art criticism most readily available. The bibliography, for example, has the following examples of books made up from articles: Apollinaire,

Baudelaire, Flanner, Fry, Geldhalzer, Greenberg, Heron, Kramer, Krauss, Liberman and Harold Rosenberg; as for lectures, some authors are Brookner, Clark, Read and Jakob Rosenberg.

To find the art critical element in other books may prove more difficult. The starred items in the bibliography are starting points for different sorts of search. Arntzen and Rainwater can be used for surveys. Standard histories like Gombrich, Gillon, Janson, Friedländer, Willett, Willetts, Hamilton, Paine and Soper (and other volumes in the Pelican History of Art series) have book lists. About artists, both Goldwater and Treves and the book by the Wittkowers make good beginnings, while Sparshott is a start for aesthetics. Johnson, Pointon and Preziosi all discuss the history of art.

Another lead into choosing books is to consult an encyclopaedia. *The Encyclopaedia of World Art* published by McGraw-Hill, for example, can be used for the book lists at the end of each article, and is valuable for monographs on those major artists who are accorded separate articles. Dictionaries of art and other reference books tend to be less helpful in leading on to other sources.

Art history is generally strong in interpretation, as books by Baxandall, Panofsky or Wind demonstrate. For descriptions, however, the reader can use catalogues, such as those cited by Davies, Levey, or catalogues raisonnés such as that by de Tolnay, or Tietze; as for evaluation, the connoisseurship of Berenson or Friedländer sets high standards. The problem of reading art history for its art critical content is that the main intention of the writer is not the same as that of the reader, who may be less interested in important historical questions absorbing to the writer.

Writings by artists are normally read for the light they throw on the artists' own work, leaving their criticism of other artists rather neglected. A similar neglect is suffered by writers, only incidentally concerned with the visual arts. Both categories of writing can have a welcome open approach which can be readily appreciated in Delacroix, Fromentin, Van Gogh, or in authors discussed by Brookner like Diderot, the brothers Goncourt, or Zola.

Critical judgements are informed by other studies; in this book's brief bibliography, philosophy is represented by Collingwood, psychology by Arnheim and Gombrich, and anthropology by Maquet. These are areas for infinite expansion. The combining of historical with artistic studies is problematic, whether concerned with the history of taste or the writings on art and society which have traditionally, as with Ruskin or Burckhardt, proposed comprehensive interpretations of a culture; rather different approaches are made by writers such as Antal, Benjamin, or Krauss.

A main challenge for the future critic is to encompass Oriental or African art, other cultures and archaeology; relevant authors cited include Gillon and Willett for Africa, Lee, Sullivan and Willetts for the Orient, and Honour and Fleming for attempting a global survey. The next decade should see many more books about unfamiliar arts, territories which are challenging for critical explorers. They will be especially interesting to read.

'Art critics are useless or harmful'; so wrote the Futurists in 1910. The calumny need not be believed. There is good reason for cautious reading of criticism, but also ample evidence of its value. Let us hope in future for more writers to match the perceptive, sensitive and eloquent critics of the past.

Bibliography

Editions listed are usually those from which quotations have been taken (but see the reference notes for details). For other lists of books and discussion of books on art, the starred items on the list are worth consulting.

ALPERS, S. *The Art of Describing*, London, 1983
ANTAL, F. *Florentine Painting and Its Social Background*. London, 1948
APOLLINAIRE, G. *The Cubist Painters*. New York, 1962
ARNHEIM, R. *Art and Visual Perception*. London, 1947
——. *The Power of the Center*. New York, 1988
* ARNTZEN, E. and RAINWATER, R. *Guide to the Literature of Art History*. Chicago, 1980
BACON, F. *Essays* (1625)
BARNES, A. *The Art of Cézanne*. New York, 1936
BARR, A. H. *Fantastic Art, Dada, Surrealism*. New York, 1936 (reprint 1947)
——. *Matisse: his art and his public*, New York, 1951
BAUDELAIRE, C. *The Mirror of Art*. London, 1955
——. *The Painter of Modern Life*. London, 1964
BAXANDALL, M. *The Limewood Sculptors of Renaissance Germany*. New Haven and London, 1980
BELL, C. *Art*. London, 1914
BENJAMIN, W. *Illuminations*. London, 1970
BERENSON, B. *Italian Painters of the Renaissance*. London, 1894–7
——. *Italian Paintings of the Renaissance*. Recent edition (7 volumes), New York, 1957–68
BROOKNER, A. *The Genius of the Future*. London, 1971
BURCKHARDT, J. *Civilization of the Renaissance in Italy*. London, 1950
BURGIN, V. *The End of Art Theory*, London, 1986
CARROLL, L. *Alice's Adventures in Wonderland*. London, 1865 (1966 edition cited)
CHADWICK, W. *Women, Art and Society*. London, 1990
CLARK, K. *Landscape into Art*. London, 1949
COLLINGWOOD, R. G. *The Principles of Art*. 1938
COOPER, D. and TINTEROW, G. *The Essential Cubism*. London, Tate Gallery, 1983
DAVIES, M. *Catalogue of the Paintings of the Earlier Italian School, the National Gallery*. London, 1951
DELACROIX, E. *Journal*. London, 1951

ELSEN, A. E. *In Rodin's Studio*. Oxford, 1980
FAGG, W. B. *African Sculpture*. London, 1970
FAURE, E. *Équivalences*. Paris, 1951
FISCHER, E. *The Necessity of Art: a Marxist Approach*. Harmondsworth, 1963
FLANNER, J. *Men and Monuments*, London, 1957
* FRIEDLÄNDER, M. *Early Netherlandish Painting from Van Eyck to Breughel*. London, 1956
FRIEDMAN, T. '*The Hyde Park Atrocity*', Leeds, 1988
FROMENTIN, E. *The Masters of Past Time*. London, 1948
FRY, R. *Vision and Design*. London, 1920
——. *Cézanne*. London, 1927
FULLER, P. *Images of God*. London, 1985
GELDHALZER, H. (ed). *New York Painting and Sculpture, 1940–1970*. London, 1969
GILLON, W. *A History of African Art*. London, 1984
GOGH, V. VAN. *The Complete Letters* (3 volumes). London, 1958
* GOLDWATER, R. and TREVES, M. *Artists on Art*. London and New York, 1949
* GOMBRICH, E. H. *The Story of Art*. London, 1950 (current enlarged edition, 1989)
——. *Art and Illusion*, London, 1960
GONCOURT, E. and J. *French Eighteenth Century Painters*. London, 1948
GREENBERG, C. *Art and Culture*. New York, 1969
HALPERN, H. U. *Félix Fénéon*. New Haven, 1988
* HAMILTON, G. H. *Painting and Sculpture in Europe, 1880–1940*. Harmondsworth, 1967
HAYTER, S. W. *About Prints*. London, 1962
HERON, P. *The Changing Forms of Art*. London, 1955
HIND, A. M. *History of Engraving and Etching*. London, revised edition, 1923
* HOLT, E. G. *A Documentary History of Art* (3 vols), New York, 1957–66
HONOUR, H. and FLEMING, J. *A World History of Art*. London, 1982
HOPE, H. R. *Georges Braque*, New York, 1949
IVINS, W. J. *How Prints Look*. New York, 1943
* JANSON, H. W. *A History of Art*. London, 1962
JEAN, M. *The History of Surrealist Painting*. London, 1960
* JOHNSON, W. McA. *Art History: Its Use and Abuse*. Toronto, 1988
* KLEINBAUER, W. E. and SLAVENS, T. P. *Research Guide to the History of Western Art*. Chicago, 1982
KRAMER, H. *The Revenge of the Philistines*. New York, 1985
KRAUSS, R. *The Originality of Modern Art and Other Modernist Myths*. New York, 1987
KUSPIT, D. *Clement Greenberg*. Madison and London, 1979
LEE, S. *A History of Far Eastern Art*. London, 1964
LESLIE, C. R. *Memoirs of the Life of John Constable*. London, 1951
LEVEY, M. *Catalogue of the Paintings of the German School, the National Gallery*. London, 1959
* ——.*The Soul of the Eye*, London, 1990
LIBERMAN, A. *The Artist in His Studio*. London, 1960
LYNTON, N., SMITH, A., CUMMING, R., and COLLINSON, D. *Looking into Paintings*. London, 1985
MALRAUX, A. *Saturn: an essay on Goya*. London, 1957
——. *Museum without Walls*. London, 1967
MAQUET, J. *The Aesthetic Experience*. New Haven and London, 1986
MASSON, G. *Companion Guide to Rome*. London, 1974
MEIER-GRAEFE, J. *Vincent*. London, 1948
MORELLI, G. *Italian Painters* (2 vols). London 1892–3
MUNRO, T. *Art Education: Its Philosophy and Psychology*. New York, 1956
NORDENFALK, C. *The Life and Work of Van Gogh*. London, 1953

NOVOTNY, F. *Painting and Sculpture in Europe 1780–1880*. Harmondsworth, 1960
* PANOFSKY, E. *Meaning in the Visual Arts*. New York, 1955
PARSONS, M. J. *How We Understand Art*. Cambridge, 1987
PATER, W. *Selected Works*. London, 1948
* POINTON, M. *History of Art: a student's handbook*. London, 1980
* PREZIOSI, D. *Rethinking Art History*. New Haven, 1989
READ, H. *The Meaning of Art*. London, 1931
——. *Art Now*. London, 1933
REES, A. L. and BORZELLO, F. (eds.) *The New Art History*, London, 1986
REYNOLDS, J. *Fifteen Discourses on Art*. London (Everyman), *c.* 1913
——. *Portraits*. London, 1952
RHEIMS, M. *The Glorious Obsession*. London, 1975
RICKETTS, C. *The Prado and Its Masterpieces* (quarto). London, 1903
ROBERTSON, B. *Jackson Pollock*. London, 1960
RODRIGUEZ, A. *A History of Mexican Mural Painting*. London, 1969
ROSENBERG, H. *The Anxious Object*. New York, 1965
ROSENBERG, J. *On Quality in Art*. New York, 1964
RUSKIN, J. *Modern Painters*. London, 1843–60 (7th edition, 1867 cited)
SAMUELS, E. *Bernard Berenson*. London, 1979
SCHAPIRO, M. *Modern Art: 19th and 20th Centuries*. London, 1978
* SPARSHOTT, F. E. *The Structure of Aesthetics*. London and Toronto, 1963
STEIN, G. *Picasso*. London, 1938
SULLIVAN, M. *Symbols of Eternity*. London, 1979
TALBOT RICE, D. *Byzantine Art*. Harmondsworth, 1935
——. *The Background of Art*. London, 1939
TAYLOR, B. *Animal Painting in Britain*. Harmondsworth, 1955
TERADA, T. *Japanese Art in World Perspective*. New York, 1976
TIETZE, H. *Tintoretto*, London, 1948
TODA, Kenji. *Japanese Scroll Painting*. Chicago, 1935
TOLNAY, C. DE. *Michelangelo* (5 volumes). New York, 1945–60
TOLSTOY, L. *What is Art?* (1898) London, 1930
TOMKINS, C. *Merchants and Masterpieces: the Story of the Metropolitan Museum of Art*. London, 1970
TRIER, E. *Form and Space*. London, 1961
VAILLANT, G. C. *The Aztecs of Mexico*. Harmondsworth, 1951
VALERY, P. *Aesthetics*. London, 1964
VASARI, G. *The Lives of the Painters, Sculptors and Architects* (4 vols). London (Everyman), 1963
VENTURI, L. *History of Art Criticism*. New York, 1936
VINCI, L. DA. *Selections from the Notebooks*. London (World's Classics), 1952
VOLLARD, A. *Paul Cézanne: His Life and Art*. New York, 1924
WILLETT, F. *African Art*. London, 1971
* WILLETTS, W. *Chinese Art* (2 vols). Harmondsworth, 1958
WIND, E. *Art and Anarchy*. London, 1963
WITT, R. C. *How to Look at Pictures*. London, 1902
* WITTKOWER, R. and M. *Born under Saturn*. London, 1963
WOLFE, T. *The Painted Word*. New York, 1975
WÖLFLINN, H. *Renaissance and Baroque*. London, 1964
ZELANSKI, P. and FISHER, M. P. *The Art of Seeing*. Englewood Cliffs, 1988

Notes

CHAPTER 1

1 Tolstoy, p. 50.
2 Pater, Walter. *Selected Works*, London, 1948, pp. 265–6.
3 Shapiro, p. 179.
4 Lucian quoted in Venturi, p. 50.
5 Fry, Roger. *Art-History as an academic study*. Cambridge, 1933, pp. 10–11.
6 Fry (1933), p. 8.
7 Pointon, p.1.
8 Kleinbauer and Stavens, p.3.
9 Ackerman, J. S. *The Historian as Critic* in Smith, R A (ed), *Aesthetics and Criticism in Art Eduction*, Chicago, 1966, p. 391.

CHAPTER 2

1 Baudelaire (1964), pp. 12–13.
2 Baudelaire (1955), p. 47.
3 Baudelaire (1964), p. 43.
4 Baudelaire (1955), p. 44.
5 Ruskin, pp. 376–8.
6 Sartre quoted in Fletcher, Valerie J, *Giacometti 1901–1966*, Washington, 1988, p. 42.
7 Apollinaire quoted in Adéma, M. *Apollinaire*, London, 1954, p. 102.
8 Apollinaire quoted in Adéma, p. 103.
9 Apollinaire quoted in Adéma, p. 104
10 Dupuy, R, quoted in Adéma, p. 153.
11 Apollinaire, Guillaume, *Oeuvres Completes* (vol 4), Paris, 1966, p. 234 (translated)
12 Apollinaire (1962), p. 20.
13 Apollinaire (1966), p. 311 (translated).
14 Stein, G. pp. 21–2.
15 Fénéon in Halpern, colour plate 3.
16 Compard, Emile, quoted in Halpern, p. 91.
17 Read, 1933, p. 164.
18 Rodriguez, p. 227, 2.18; Fischer, p. 108.

19 Lu Hsun in Sullivan, p. 180.
20 Mao Tse-tung in Sullivan, p. 180.
21 Barr, p. 9.
22 Barr, p. 11.
23 Barr, p. 9.
24 Reynolds (Everyman), p. 67.
25 Reynolds (Everyman), p. 69.
26 Reynolds (1952), p 132.
27 Blake, W, quoted in Goldwater and Treves, p. 259.
28 Valéry, P, quoted in Kramer, p. 98.
29 Burgin, p. 31.
30 Krauss, p. 247.
31 Krauss, p. 258.

CHAPTER 3

1 Carroll, p. 166.
2 Burckhardt, p. x.
3 Janson, p. 507.
4 Janson, p. 445.
5 Lee, p. 117.
6 Wölflinn (1964), p. xi.
7 Murray, P, in Wölflinn (1964), pp. 7–8.
8 Faure quoted in Picon, G, *Panorama des idées contemporaines*, Paris, 1957, p. 369 (translated).
9 Wind, p. 77.
10 Shelley, P B, qoted in Singleton, E, *Great Pictures as seen and described by Great Writers*, New York, 1900, p. 287–8.
11 Baedeker Guide to Central Italy, London, 1909, p. xvii.
12 Baedeker (1909), p. 376.
13 Masson, p. 464.
14 Paine, R T, in Paine and Soper, p. 2.
15 Hind, p. 81.
16 Hind, p. 71.
17 Baxandall, p. 48.
18 Baxandall, p. 206.
19 Ivins, p. 3.
20 Ivins, pp. 126–7.
21 Matisse, H, in Barr, p. 122.
22 Vaillant, p. 156.
23 Clark (1953), pp. xviii–xix.
24 Clark (1953), p. 83.
25 Waterhouse, E H, quoted in Taylor, p. 12.
26 Chadwick, p. 11.
27 Chadwick, p. 12.
28 Talbot Rice, p. 27.

CHAPTER 4

1 Fry (1927), p. 1.
2 Fry (1927), p. 3.
3 Fry (1927), p. 65.
4 Fry (1927), pp. 69–70.
5 Fry (1927), p. 49.
6 Vollard, p. 138.
7 Wittkower, p. xxiii–xxiv.
8 Leslie, p. 72.
9 Nordenfalk, p. 9.
10 Nordenfalk, p. 125.

11 Meier-Graefe, p. 7.
12 Gainsborough, T, quoted in Goldwater and Treves, p. 189.
13 Lawrence, T, quoted in Goldwater and Treves, p. 192.
14 Cole, T, quoted in Goldwater and Treves, p. 281.
15 Delacroix, E, quoted in Goldwater and Treves, p. 229.
16 Delacroix, E, quoted in Goldwater and Treves, p. 231.
17 Hamilton, p. 33.
18 Elsen, p. 25.
19 Gleichen, Lord Edward, quoted in Friedman, p. 141.

CHAPTER 5

1 Morelli (vol 1), p. 79.
2 This account is based on Highet, G, *The Art of Teaching*, London, pp. 212–4.
3 Morelli quoted in Samuels, p. 103.
4 Berenson (1894), p. vii.
5 Berenson quoted in Samuels, p. 105.
6 Tietze, p. 358.
7 Hilton, Tim in *Picasso's Picassos*, London. 1981, p. 80.
8 *The Shock of Recognition*, London, Tate Gallery, 1971, no. 63.
9 Stein, Judith E. in *Making their Mark*, New York, 1989, p. 81.
10 McEvilley, Thomas in Stein (1989), p. 187.
11 Colvin, Sidney, *Burne Jones*, London, Leicester Gallery, 1904, n.p.
12 Fletcher (1988), p. 171.
13 Berthoud in Fletcher (1988), p. 16.
14 Lynton, Norbert, *Ken Kiff*, London, Fischer Gallery, 1988, n.p.
15 Davies, p. 42.
16 Levey, p. 19.
17 Tomkins, p. 133.
18 Fuller, p. 71.
19 Barnes (1939), p. 39.
20 Cooper, p. 90.
21 Rheims, p. 244.

CHAPTER 6

1 Kramer, p. 110.
2 Kramer, p. 101.
3 Heron, p. 81.
4 Liberman, p. 9.
5 Liberman, p. 38.
6 Flanner, p. 190.
7 Diderot in Tollemache, B L, *Diderot's Thoughts on Art and Style*. London, 1893, pp. 127–8.
8 Sainte Beuve in Tollemache, pp. 23–4.
9 Wolfe, pp. 4–6.
10 Wolfe, p. 28.
11 Kuspit, p. 3.
12 Reise, B, in Kuspit, p. 4.
13 Greenberg C, in Geldzhahler, p. 361.
14 Burgin, p. 204.

CHAPTER 7

1 Trier, p. 59.
2 Vasari (Everyman vol 1), p. 69.
3 Goncourt, p. 127.
4 Willett, p. 144.
5 Vinci (World's Classics), pp. 118–19.
6 Vasari (Everyman vol 1), pp. 231–2 and 239.

7 Willetts (vol 2), p. 616.
8 Willetts (vol 2), p. 616.
9 Parsons, p. 22.
10 Torada, pp. 150–1.
11 Maquet, p. 164.

CHAPTER 8

1 Panofsky, pp. 30 and 32.
2 Stein (1989), p. 88.
3 Jean, p. 128.
4 Fry (1920), p. 50.
5 Rosenfield, J M, *The Courtly Tradition in Japanese Art and Literature: selections from the Hofer and Hyde collections*, Fogg Art Museum, Harvard University, 1973, p. 264.
6 Toda, p. 5.
7 Robertson, pp. 92 and 95.
8 Sverakova, Slavka in *Alexander MacLennan: Is/No,* Bristol, Arnolfini Gallery, 1988, p. 59.
9 Meyerowitz, Eva, in *Burlington Magazine*, LXXXII, pp. 31–6.

CHAPTER 9

1 Novotny, p. 79.
2 Ricketts, p. 65.
3 Malraux, pp. 35 and 179.
4 *Treasures of Tutenkhamun,* British Museum, London, 1973, p. 34.
5 Gillon, p. 82.
6 Bell, p. 27.
7 Talbot Rice (1939), p. 150.
8 Willetts (vol 2), p. 269.
9 Clark (1953), p. 36.
10 Delacroix quoted in Binyon, Mrs L, *The Mind of the Artist,* London, 1909, p. 13.
11 Bingham quoted in McCourbrey, J W, *American Art 1700–1960*, Englewood Cliffs, 1965, p. 148
12 Delacroix quoted in Binyon (1909), pp. 137–8.
13 Moore in Herbert, R L, *Modern Artists on Art*, Englewood Cliffs, 1964, p. 142.
14 Gasquet, J, *Cézanne*, Paris, 1921, p. 101 (translated).
15 Wolff quoted in Bulley, M H, *Art and Counterfeit*, London, 1925, pp. 68–9.
16 Fouquier quoted in Vollard, p. 187.
17 Guillemot quoted in Vollard, p. 204.
18 Dickens quoted in Bulley (1925), p. 68.
19 Delacroix quoted in Binyon (1909), p. 7.
20 Lavalleye, J, *Introduction aux Etudes d'Archaeologie et d'Histoire de l'Art,* Louvain and Paris, 1958, p. 26 (translated).
21 Brookner, p. 1.

CHAPTER 10

1 Bacon in his essay on *Studies*.
2 Gilpin quoted in Sparshott, p. 326.
3 Panofsky, p. 329.
4 Rosenberg, pp. 123–4.
5 Fromentin, pp. 196–7.
6 Gerson in Fromentin, p. xiii.
7 Braque in Hope, p. 146.

Index